8 Old Testament Passages That Changed the World

D1339182

8 Old Testament Passages That Changed the World

Joseph Bentz

THE FOUNDRY
PUBLISHING®

Copyright © 2021 by Joseph Bentz
The Foundry Publishing®
PO Box 419527
Kansas City, MO 64141
thefoundrypublishing.com

ISBN 978-0-8341-4031-8

Printed in the
United States of America

Cover design: J.R. Caines
Interior design: Sharon Page

Library of Congress Cataloging-in-Publication Data
Names: Bentz, Joseph, 1961- author.
Title: 8 Old Testament passages that changed the world / Joseph Bentz.
Other titles: Eight Old Testament passages that changed the world
Description: Kansas City, MO : The Foundry Publishing, [2021] | Includes bibliographical references. | Summary:
  "The author explores 8 Old Testament passages that have shaped, and continue to shape, our lives in profound ways, and helps the readers discover in them new meaning for their lives. The book looks at the ways culture has treated, mistreated, distorted, and brought to life the most well-known portions of the Old Testament, and asks why they have such a grip in every arena of life"—Provided by publisher.
Identifiers: LCCN 2021027364 | ISBN 9780834140318 (paperback) | ISBN 9780834140325 (ebook)
Subjects: LCSH: Bible. Old Testament—Criticism, interpretation, etc. | Bible. Old Testament—Influence.
Classification: LCC BS1171.3 .B396 2021 | DDC 221.6—dc23
LC record available at https://lccn.loc.gov/2021027364

10 9 8 7 6 5 4 3 2 1

Contents

CONTENTS

8 Old Testament Passages
That Changed the World

1

Torah scroll of Jewish community in Kaifeng, China // American Bible Society

The Old Testament—
Who Needs It?

THE "OLD TESTAMENT." Consider that name for a moment. Looking purely from the perspective of reader appeal, that title doesn't sound like it has much going for it, does it? "Old." Who wants that? Doesn't that imply there must be one that is newer and better? Why not just skip this old thing and move on to the new one, the New Testament? One translation of the Old Testament even addresses that "old" problem, calling it the *First Testament*. Some scholars prefer to call it the Hebrew Bible.

But the name is not the only thing about this book that is daunting. For readers today, so much of the Old Testament feels distant and confusing, and sometimes even offensive. God comes across as so mean and inexplicable in so many places. All that war and violence, and entire kingdoms getting wiped out. What is a reader today supposed to do with all that? And what about all those prophecies that are so bewildering—Joel, Habakkuk, Nahum—talking about people and places so unfamiliar to us now? Should we even be reading it? The Old Testament might be easier to handle if it were one book following one clear story line, but instead it's a head-spinning *collection* of texts—poetry, history, biography, prophecy, law, songs, proverbs—and who knows what else.

Even the parts that are understandable, the parts that make good Sunday school lessons for kids, still raise lots of questions. Jonah inside a big whatever-kind-of-fish for three days? A serpent *speaking* to Adam and Eve? A flood that wipes out everything except Noah and his family and those animals in the big boat? What about Job, suffering because of a wager between God and Satan? What do we make of all this?

The Bible has its heroes, but even they seem so flawed. David slays the giant, and we all cheer. He conquers one danger after another and becomes king. He's a man after God's own heart, we're told. But then he goes and has that secret affair with Bathsheba and plots to get her husband killed in the war in order to cover up his own bad actions. So what should we think of David? Hero? Villain? And he's one of the best kings. So many of the others we read about are pure evil. The people they lead, God's chosen people, are not much better much of the time. They keep falling away from God, turning to idols and pushing God and his prophets to the brink.

The Old Testament gives us laws such as "Thou shalt not kill" and "Thou shalt not steal," but what about all those other laws—hundreds of them—about clothing and animals and skin diseases? What do we do with those?

Christians—which is what I am—believe the Old Testament is part of God's Word, so it feels disrespectful to express these uncomfortable thoughts too directly. That's why many Christians keep quiet about such reservations. Instead, they show respect for the Old Testament and simply pick and choose from the nicer sections of it, like Psalm 23, and pretty much leave the rest alone. After all, how much do Christians really need it? We've got the *New* Testament! The words of Jesus! The letters of Paul! Sure, the Old Testament was fine for its day, but isn't it time to move on?

In fact, many Christians essentially *have* moved on from the Old Testament. In his book *The Old Testament Is Dying*, Brent A. Strawn writes that for many churches and individual Christians today, the Old Testament mostly has stopped being treated as authoritative in the spiritual lives of believers. These individuals and churches "do not regard the Old Testament in the same way (or as highly) as the New Testament, do not understand the Old Testament, would prefer to do without the Old Testament, and for all practical purposes do exactly that by means of their neglect and ignorance of it, whether in private devotion or public worship or both."[1]

One sign of the diminishing influence of the Old Testament in churches today is the number of sermons preached out of Old Testament texts. Strawn offers evidence from the Pew Forum's "U.S. Religious Knowledge Survey," released in 2010, which includes an analysis of seventy-one years of "Best Sermons" collections published in the twentieth century. During those years, 49 percent of the 879 sermons use the New Testament alone, while only 21 percent use the Old Testament alone. Perhaps even more surprisingly, 23 percent of the sermons use no biblical text at all.[2]

Even the sermons that focus on the Old Testament tend to be restricted to select popular texts while ignoring the other books. Psalms, Genesis, Exodus, Isaiah, and Jeremiah are used most frequently. Some people get their Old Testament knowledge secondhand, such as from hymns or choruses. However, Strawn cites one study that shows that in hymnals published since 1985, 64 of the 150 psalms are never mentioned. Other studies indicate that many songs that do make use of the psalms distort their meanings. Yet many Christians believe they "know" the psalms based on these songs.[3] Why bother reading and studying them for ourselves when the songwriters have already translated them into a form that somewhat approximates their original meaning? We're all set!

And Yet, We Can't Get Away from It

With so much pessimism about the Old Testament's status today, even within the church, why write a book about it? While I agree with Strawn and others that the Old Testament faces many assaults and challenges in our day, I also see ways in which its influence is still around us, and its power makes it as relevant as ever.

Let's imagine you don't even like the Old Testament and do your best to avoid it at all costs. Does that mean it hasn't shaped you? If I say "commandments," what number are you most likely to associate with it? If I say "Goliath," what name do you immediately want to pair with it? If I say "Jonah," what animal pops into your head? If I say "_____ and the ark," what name do you put in the blank?

These Old Testament stories and passages show up in places the original writers could never have imagined: television commercials, social media memes, movies, novels, paintings, sculptures, ad copy, jokes, cigarette packaging, children's books, songs, poems, news articles, protest signs, court cases, college textbooks, toys, wallpaper, and many other places. This book looks at the many ways culture has treated, mistreated, distorted, and brought to life the most well-known portions of the Old Testament. Taking the passages that are inescapable, this book asks why those words and stories continue to have such a grip on every area of life. If these words hold such power over us now, what could we learn from them if we delved into them even deeper?

This book's approach doesn't replace other ways of experiencing the Old Testament. It doesn't replace commentaries, textbooks, devotionals, or sermons. Each of those ways of probing the complex and fascinating text of the Old Testament is useful. Each can reveal a dimension of the text that no other method can. This book is simply another point of entry into the Old Testament world, with an emphasis on the countless ways these passages have made indelible impressions on the everyday lives and cultures of our own generation and those that have come before.

The Old Testament provokes a variety of responses from people today. Some ignore it altogether. Some revere it but don't bother to read it. Some embrace it and probe its meaning. Some trash it and try to use its contents to discredit the faith of those who believe it as the Word of God. How much do these Old Testament critics dislike it and the God who is portrayed in it? One of the most frequently quoted criticisms comes from the prominent atheist writer Richard Dawkins, who wrote, "The God of the Old Testament is arguably the most unpleasant character of all fiction: jealous and proud of it; a petty, unjust, unforgiving control-freak; a vindictive, bloodthirsty ethnic cleanser; a misogynistic, homophobic, racist, infanticidal, genocidal, filicidal, pestilential, megalomaniacal, sadomasochistic, capriciously malevolent bully."[4] Whew! That is certainly not the God I learned about in Sunday school. It does not describe the God I serve today. However, I have read plenty of disturbing episodes in the Old Testament, stories that make some of God's actions look inexplicable if not outright mean. What do I do with such scenes? Is Dawkins right?

When it comes to reading ancient texts, many forces can lead to misunderstanding. As I will show throughout this book, the same outlets of popular culture that keep these Old Testament passages in people's minds also distort those passages. If people see and hear enough commercials, cartoons, movies, and other genres that parody a biblical story, the parody can stick in people's minds far more vividly than the original text, which many people have never read for themselves anyway. How many people think, for instance, that Eve ate an apple? No apples appear in Genesis, but that fruit is almost universally associated with the Adam and Eve story.

That particular distortion of an Old Testament story may be harmless, but other distortions, stereotypes, and misunderstandings may twist people's perceptions not only of the Bible but also of God himself. People may even turn against God or stay away from him in the first place because of these misunderstandings about what even the most well-known passages say.

It is hard, perhaps impossible at times, to fully enter and understand a text the way the original readers did. We try to throw our minds back to those eras we are reading about, but our own perspectives are so strong, and our own knowledge of the details of past cultures is so limited, that we have to admit there are almost certainly nuances we are missing, if not major concepts that could significantly alter the work's meaning.

To see how this distortion happens, I don't even have to go to ancient texts. As a literature professor, I see it happen with books from the relatively recent past. One of the novels I teach in my American literature course is Kate Chopin's *The Awakening*, published in 1899. The novel is set in New Orleans and on Grand Isle in the Gulf of Mexico. The wealthy families spend summers on Grand Isle rather than in their New Orleans mansions. When I ask students why the rich people of that day would do that, most give answers that make more sense for today than for the world of a little more than a hundred years ago. Maybe the rich wanted a change of scenery, or they thought it would be fun to be on the beach, or that's just what rich people do. Those are possible motivations, but few of my students have ever offered the more urgent reason that wealthy families fled to the Gulf breezes in the summer: to escape disease.

We discuss the prevalence of mosquitoes in that area, which brought cholera, yellow fever, and other illnesses. We also talk about what New Orleans would have been like in an era when horses—and the hundreds of thousands of pounds of manure they produced each year—would have filled the streets. In cities across America in those days, dried horse manure created a haze that hung in the air and caused breathing problems. In rainy seasons, horse manure could turn roads into muddy swamps, which could also become breeding grounds for mosquitoes. Workers tried tirelessly to clean up the endless messes, but the staggering load of manure was often dumped into rivers, polluting those too. No wonder the rich wanted a summertime escape from this smelly, disease-ridden mess.

None of those details, however, are mentioned in the novel. Why not? The original readers would have taken those muddy, hazy, manure-covered, mosquito-laden conditions for granted. Novelists didn't need to describe the obvious, just as a novelist today wouldn't spend any time describing the electric light bulbs that illuminate a room, the air-conditioning that cools a room, or the hundred other everyday details that may be very different a hundred or a thousand years from now. That omission makes sense for readers today, because who would want the good plot of a novel slowed down by a description of air-conditioning? But readers several generations from now may misread a scene because of it. Novelists also omit explanations of other cultural references, such as movies, songs, or television shows. Today's readers may understand the references, but readers twenty or fifty years from now will need a footnote to make sense of them. I teach a short story that mentions Johnny Carson, a person nearly everyone in my own generation knows, but for many of my students, his is an unfamiliar name.

If readers have trouble recognizing and understanding cultural references from within the past fifty years, then how much more difficult it will be for them to fully make sense of biblical texts written a few thousand years ago? The amazing thing may be that people still connect to these stories. As I observed earlier, people today not only embrace those ancient stories but also can't resist retelling them in new genres, new art forms, using technologies the original storytellers never could have imagined: film, television, social media, and others. These new ways of telling the old stories keep them alive in our culture, but each retelling, as I also noted, risks creating and compounding false stereotypes and misinformation about the Old Testament.

David T. Lamb is one scholar who has confronted the negative stereotypes of God's portrayal in the Old Testament. His book *God Behaving Badly* challenges the charges that God is angry, sexist, racist, violent, legalistic, rigid, and distant. The God of the Old Testament is the same God as in the New Testament, and he is loving and just. Some well-known Old Testament passages, however, make that hard to see at first.

Take the issue of God's anger. In cartoons, jokes, and many people's perceptions, the God of the Old Testament is often seen as the gray-bearded, angry deity who is ready to strike people with lightning at the first sign of disobedience. He is a grouchy, old grandpa or the crazy next-door neighbor, scarily lashing out at anyone who crosses him. Is that the truth of Scripture? Lamb shows that a careful analysis of each case of God's anger paints a much different portrait. God does show anger, but he uses it in ways that are ultimately protective of his people.

Take one of the famous Old Testament stories of God's anger, a story that never made much sense to me and that appeared to put God in a bad light. David and thirty thousand chosen men of Israel were transporting the ark of the covenant to Jerusalem on a cart. Along the way, they were celebrating before the Lord, and "Uzzah reached out and took hold of the ark of God, because the oxen stumbled. The LORD's anger burned against Uzzah because of his irreverent act; therefore God struck him down, and he died there beside the ark of God" (2 Samuel 6:6-7).

Why did God do this? Why did he angrily kill Uzzah for trying to keep the ark from falling off the cart? Doesn't that show God to be a petulant, angry, legalistic deity? That's how it looked to me. But Lamb shows that

God's actions make sense—and in the long run are protective of his people— if you examine the situation more carefully. "Handling the ark was inherently dangerous," writes Lamb, "like handling radioactive materials. If people do not use proper precaution when transporting plutonium, people die."[5] The Nuclear Regulatory Commission, he points out, gives far more rules about handling radioactive material than the Bible does about handling the ark. It's easy to understand the strictness with radioactive substances, but why is God so picky about the ark? God's presence, while loving and protective, is also dangerous. Think of how careful Moses and the Hebrew people had to be, and the boundaries they had to observe, at the foot of the mountain where God delivered the Ten Commandments. The ark represented God's presence and therefore was not to be treated lightly.

Careful instructions for how the ark was to be carried were given to the people, as several passages of Scripture indicate, but the people were ignoring them. The ark was not supposed to be riding on a cart. It was designed to be lifted and carried with two parallel poles that fit into rings on the side of the ark. That method of transportation was built into the very design of it. Priests were to carry it, and the method offered safety, since no one would have to touch the ark. It also showed respect, since that method mirrored the way royalty or other honored persons were transported.

The ark represented not only God but also the covenant between him and the Israelites. It was a relationship they had repeatedly abused. Their carelessness and wrongdoing had already caused them to lose the ark to the Philistines. Now that it was rescued, would they take their covenant with God more seriously and follow his commands? This movement of the ark had an audience of thirty thousand Israelites. Lamb explains that God "valued the covenant with his people so highly that he wanted to communicate the message that he would not tolerate disrespect for the object that symbolized that relationship."[6] The punishment was harsh, but it served as a deterrent. The ark was treated with respect from that time forward, and such punishment did not have to be repeated.

Lamb takes a similar approach in his treatment of other distorted images of God that can emerge—mistakenly or deliberately—as modern readers confront the Old Testament. He writes, "As we become aware of the context of the Old Testament, the problematic portrayals of Yahweh don't magically disappear, but they do become more understandable. And as we study the cultural contexts alongside the numerous passages that portray Yahweh more favorably, not only does a highly attractive God emerge, but God's followers also appear as people we would want to emulate, not as hotheads, chauvinists and bigots."[7]

A Book That Can't Be Judged by Our Own Limitations

While it may be true that God and the Old Testament do not conform to all the negative stereotypes placed upon them, that does not change the fact that the Old Testament is a weird, wonderful, disturbing, fascinating book. Who can fully understand it or come to terms with it? Even scholars who devote their lives to studying it never get to the end of what needs to be said about it.

No matter how many times we wind our way through the Old Testament's poetry, history, prophecy, biography, songs, laws, speeches, miracle stories, and words of wisdom, we will never reach the point when we can honestly say, "Now I get it. Now I have mined the depths of what this text has to offer and have mastered it." What was obscure when we were twenty may seem clear when we are fifty, but the text we thought we had nailed down at age twenty may break open new questions when we're fifty.

I'm in favor of anything—scholarly, artistic, musical, devotional—that can help me understand the Old Testament better, but I also acknowledge there are limits to my understanding. Why should the God of the universe, and the book that describes his actions in ancient times, make complete sense to me? Why should his actions conform to my twenty-first-century expectations?

Wouldn't it be more likely that many things about him and this book would be *beyond* my comprehension? Wouldn't a being as magnificent as God naturally be so far above me that a certain amount of coming to terms with him would have to come through trust rather than understanding? When I was a child, I found my parents incomprehensible in many ways. Their endless restrictions about where I couldn't wander, what I couldn't climb, what I couldn't eat, and so on seemed arbitrary and mean when I was three years old. Why couldn't I just do what I wanted to do? What could possibly go wrong? I later realized why it was a bad idea to wander into the street or why it could be harmful to try to eat that fascinating cigarette butt plucked from the pavement. Later in life, I would place the same restrictions on my own uncomprehending children.

Maybe it is irresistible to try to judge the God of the Old Testament, and to judge the book itself, according to our own limited understanding of the universe. As a three-year-old, I couldn't fully understand my parents, and I couldn't talk them out of their actions that didn't meet my approval. I did love them, I learned to trust them, and I gained increasing understanding of them. Like many other people, I have a strong sense of how God should behave and how I would behave if I were in his shoes. He doesn't always meet my expectations. What should I do about that?

In a social media age of instant moral judgments, when everyone with a Twitter account feels justified in becoming the moral arbiter of the actions and words of every celebrity, politician, athlete, or regular person anywhere, it's easy to expect God to also conform to our own limited vision of what he should do. He doesn't. Rejecting him is one possible response to that dilemma. Many people have chosen that. Another possible response is to ignore or set aside the Old Testament in favor of ideas about God that feel more palatable, in the New Testament or elsewhere. Many people have done that.

One more option is to let the Old Testament open a door to the mystery God reveals himself to be. I once thought that intently studying the Old Testament might help me comprehend God better. Through such study, I would gain a clearer sense of how he operates and what I should expect from him. I discovered something much different. God is not so easily captured and mastered. The Bible shows him in action but does not encompass him. He is unpredictable, strange, beyond my explaining. I can learn about him from the words of Scripture, but I cannot reduce him to my comprehension. In fact, just the opposite happens. Rather than solving the mystery of who God is, the Old Testament cracks open the door of his vast mystery. He is not the God I thought I knew. He is more. That should not surprise me. Even those to whom God revealed himself most intimately didn't fully understand him, such as Moses, David, Adam and Eve, and Abraham.

God is not the only figure in the Old Testament who is portrayed in a far more complex way than might be expected. The "heroes" of Scripture are pretty surprising too. They often behave in ways that are far from heroic, yet God does not abandon them. Instead, they are exactly the people he calls on to help fulfill his purposes. Out of all the humans he had to choose from, couldn't God have picked some who were a little less corrupt, violent, womanizing, and impulsive?

Chad Bird, in his spiritual memoir, *Night Driving: Notes from a Prodigal Soul*, asks why Scripture airs so much dirty laundry, and he imagines what the Old Testament would be like if it were rewritten to leave out the embarrassing episodes. What if Adam and Eve didn't eat the forbidden fruit, Joseph's brothers didn't betray him, Noah didn't get drunk, Aaron didn't make the golden calf, David didn't have his affair with Bathsheba, and so on?

The message that such a heavily edited Old Testament would send, says Bird, "is the same message we want to believe about ourselves: that the spiritual life is about being strong, not weak; victorious, not defeated; standing tall, not humbled low. This rewritten Bible would affirm the widespread delusion that the masks of strength we wear in public are part of the God-pleasing, standard-issue uniform of the faithful."[8] One reason the heroes of the Old Testament are so approachable is that their foibles are so recognizable. We may find that we share some of them. They are insecure. They are lustful. They doubt God. They act rashly. They try to cover up their sin.

In the end, God exposes them for who they are. As Bird puts it, "[God] was at work in their lives to reveal not how strong they were, but how very weak. Through these stories, he opens our eyes not to some hidden reservoir of integrity within us, but to the swamp of vice inside us all."[9] He does this not to destroy them, but to save them. They can't turn from their sin if they don't see it, and neither can we. The message of the Old Testament, then, is in this way the same as the message of the New Testament: only God can save us.

Bird, like many of us, learned this message the hard way. He didn't truly understand the Old Testament until his life fell apart. Because of an affair, Bird, who had been a pastor and professor, lost his wife, family, and job. He became a truck driver, and that's when he approached the Old Testament anew, starting with the book of Psalms, as he read it during long nights on the road in his truck. The psalms offered him what he needed, a language he could use to cry out to God. "The Psalms place words on our lips so critical of God they border on blasphemy," he writes. "They translate our suffering into speech, yes, but they also translate God's seeming absence into a surprising presence. The Psalms reveal a God who, though he feels worlds away from us, is as close as the marrow in our bones."[10] He prayed those psalms to God, not serenely, but in desperation, hurling them at God.

In this way, the Old Testament, even in its most bizarre, bewildering passages, can be life giving. It challenges every stereotype of God that anyone could come up with. He shocks us. He loves us. He reveals himself but also conceals himself. He frightens us, but he also rescues us. That is why, a few thousand years after these passages were written, we still can't leave them alone.

This book doesn't cover all the important passages of the Old Testament. No single book could. There are many other passages I wish I had room to delve into. I focused particularly on stories, people, and passages that have had a profound influence on various aspects of popular entertainment, the arts, law, the church, and individual lives. *Why* is the question I asked most frequently as I wrote this book. Why has this particular story meant so much to people? Why has this passage spawned films, memes, jokes, paintings, sculptures, and endless retellings?

The chapters are not in the order in which they appear in the Old Testament. I start with the story of David because it explodes with all the Old Testament has to offer—drama, emotional intensity, action, spiritual depth, success and failure, and the forward movement of the larger story that God is unfolding throughout the entire range of Scripture.

I started this introductory chapter with indications of the declining influence of the Old Testament, but I believe its stories, themes, and truths have never been more relevant. It inspires, instructs, delights, and shocks. It points the way to life. I invite you to dive into it with me as we consider what a difference this book can make.

Notes

1. Brent A. Strawn, *The Old Testament Is Dying: A Diagnosis and Recommended Treatment* (Grand Rapids: Baker Academic, 2017), 5.

2. Strawn, 30.

3. Strawn, 39-40.

4. Richard Dawkins, *The God Delusion* (New York: Mariner, 2008), 51.

5. David T. Lamb, *God Behaving Badly: Is the God of the Old Testament Angry, Sexist and Racist?* (Downers Grove, IL: IVP, 2011), 28.

6. Lamb, 32.

7. Lamb, 23.

8. Chad Bird, *Night Driving: Notes from a Prodigal Soul* (Grand Rapids: Eerdmans, 2017), 84.

9. Bird, 91.

10. Bird, 38.

Digging Deeper

1. This chapter gives evidence of the diminishing influence of the Old Testament in our day, but it also shows ways in which it still plays a significant role culturally and in people's individual lives. What part does the Old Testament play in your own life? How much do you see its influence in the culture in which you live?

2. What stereotypes are there of the God of the Old Testament? In what ways does this chapter challenge those ideas? How convincing are those explanations? How much *should* we humans expect to comprehend about God and what he is like?

3. The Old Testament has "heroes," but most of them are flawed, and some of them are *very* flawed. What impact do these less-than-admirable traits have on how you see those biblical figures? Why do you think the Old Testament texts give so much attention to those imperfections?

Go to https://www.thefoundrypublishing.com/8OT/LeaderGuide for a free downloadable leader's guide that includes more questions for reflection as well as activities for use in a small group setting.

2

David Slaying Goliath // Pietro da Cortona // c. 1596–1669

David Slays a Giant— but Not All of Them

*45 David said to the Philistine, "You come against me with sword and spear and jav-
elin, but I come against you in the name of the LORD Almighty, the God of the armies of
Israel, whom you have defied. 46 This day the LORD will deliver you into my hands, and I'll
strike you down and cut off your head. This very day I will give the carcasses of the Philistine army to the birds and the wild animals, and the whole world will know that there is a
God in Israel. 47 All those gathered here will know that it is not by sword or spear that the
LORD saves; for the battle is the LORD's, and he will give all of you into our hands."*

*48 As the Philistine moved closer to attack him, David ran quickly toward the battle
line to meet him. 49 Reaching into his bag and taking out a stone, he slung it and struck
the Philistine on the forehead. The stone sank into his forehead, and he fell facedown on
the ground.*

*50 So David triumphed over the Philistine with a sling and a stone; without a sword in
his hand he struck down the Philistine and killed him.*

—1 Samuel 17:45-50

IS IT ANY WONDER that the story of David and Goliath has fired the
imaginations of people around the world for centuries? The story has
something for everyone. On the high end of the cultural scale, it inspired
one of the most artistically renowned statues in history—Michelangelo's
David—in 1504. On the less exalted side of pop culture nearly five hundred years later, the animated *Veggie Tales* film "Dave and the Giant Pickle"
emerged, in which the underdog Dave, played by an asparagus, takes on
the giant pickle Goliath.

One sign of a story's cultural power is when it transcends the story itself
to become a metaphor. Even if you have never read the story in the Bible,
chances are you still know what people mean when they call something a
"David and Goliath" situation. Businesses that are small but scrappy refer
to their "David versus Goliath" quest to outdo the bloated companies that
are their competitors. Underdog sports teams who achieve victories over
sure-winner opponents revel in their David versus Goliath status. Self-help
gurus call on people to find their inner David who can vanquish the men-
tal and circumstantial Goliaths holding them back. Goliath can represent
almost any "giant": poverty, excessive weight, perfectionism, abuse, self-
doubt, outdated thinking, and so on.

If you want to read the original story of David and Goliath, the Bible
tells it beautifully and economically. The battle itself takes up only two
verses, 1 Samuel 17:48-49, and the entire story fits easily into chapter 17.

Most people, however, encounter the story in someone else's retelling of it before they ever read it in Scripture. If you attended Sunday school as a child, you probably heard the story multiple times. Dozens of children's books tell it. For centuries, adults have experienced retellings of it in poetry, sermons, novels, films, and paintings.

Like other classic stories, the account of David and Goliath opens itself up in new ways to writers and artists of every generation. Creative individuals of each era retell it from their own points of view, and in those retellings they also partially redefine the story. They find ways to appropriate it for their own artistic or literary or self-help or commercial purposes. What is it about this story that makes it so enduring? Why such interest in a brave young man who, armed with a sling and some stones, slays a large, heavily armed foe that everyone else was too afraid to fight?

As we will see, the story is only one episode in the life of one of the most fascinating and complex figures not only in the Bible but also in all of history—King David. Steven L. McKenzie, who wrote a biography of David, observes that the Bible "devotes more space to David than to any other character. Moses and Jesus rival him for sheer number of pages until you add the Psalms. Then David wins hands down. But even without the Psalms, there is more about David's life than about the lives of the other biblical characters."[1] David accomplishes this heroic deed of killing Goliath when he is still young and unknown. He will go on to other great acts, but he will also go on to commit less admirable, even despicable, acts. He will become a murderer, a philanderer, a fugitive, a poet, and a king. But before we get to all that, before we consider how, in spite of all the blemishes on his life, he still came to be called "a man after [God's] own heart" (1 Samuel 13:14; Acts 13:22), let's first probe this most famous of the stories of David, his killing of Goliath, to see what it is about the story that makes it so irresistible.

The Ultimate Underdog

One reason people love this story so much is that David is the ultimate underdog. He is the little guy that everyone overlooks. No one takes him seriously or expects much from him.

Before David emerges onto the scene in 1 Samuel, King Saul has proved unfaithful, so God decides to replace him. He calls on Samuel, the judge, to go see Jesse in Bethlehem. The Lord has chosen a king among Jesse's sons. But which son?

Jesse has plenty of sons to choose from. Seven of them are lined up to walk past Samuel, and they all look fine to him. But the Lord has a different idea. After the first candidate, the Lord tells Samuel, "Do not consider his appearance or his height, for I have rejected him. The LORD does not look at the things people look at. People look at the outward appearance, but the LORD looks at the heart" (1 Samuel 16:7). Samuel has to reject all seven of these sons because the Lord has not chosen them.

Then, in a Cinderella moment, Samuel asks whether there might be any other sons lurking somewhere. Only the youngest one, says Jesse. But he's out tending the sheep. No one would have expected the youngest son to be chosen, so why bother putting him in the lineup? But as soon as young David is brought to them, the Lord tells Samuel to rise and anoint him, for this is the one. Samuel anoints him, "and from that day on the Spirit of the LORD came powerfully upon David" (v. 13).

The Spirit of the Lord also departs from Saul, but he is not deposed immediately. In fact, David becomes his armor-bearer. David plays the lyre for him and soothes Saul's troubled mind. Saul is deteriorating. David is rising.

Enter the Philistines, enemy of the Israelites. The Philistine army gathers on one mountain, and the Israelite army waits on the opposite mountain, and a valley separates them. Now we get a glimpse of the Philistine champion, Goliath. If the story were a movie, it would fit the action/adventure genre, with an emphasis on the oversized villain. Experts are divided on Goliath's height. Some scholars say he is up to ten feet tall. Others estimate his height at closer to seven feet. During the fight, he will wear about 150 pounds of body armor, including a bronze helmet. He will carry a spear with a 19-pound spearhead, not to mention a bronze javelin and a sword. That doesn't leave him any free hands to carry a shield, so he has a shield bearer who walks in front of him.

This giant of a man throws out a challenge. If an Israelite will fight him and kill him, the Philistines will become the Israelites' servants. If Goliath kills the Israelite, the Israelites will serve the Philistines. Who is ready to fight?

The Israelites are afraid. David's three eldest brothers are fighting for Saul, but they don't step up. David goes back and forth between his shepherd duties and the gathering of soldiers. No one considers him as a possible combatant. He's not a soldier. His father has him take food to his brothers.

The standoff continues for forty days, as Goliath comes forward daily to taunt the Israelites with his challenge. Finally, David can't take it anymore. He speaks up. "What will be done for the man who kills this Philistine and removes this disgrace from Israel? Who is this uncircumcised Philistine that he should defy the armies of the living God?" (17:26). His question brings only mockery. David's eldest brother angrily tells him to get back to his sheep.

King Saul eventually catches wind of David's interest, and he sends for him. The king tells David he's just a boy and can't fight Goliath. But David doesn't give up. He may be only a shepherd, he says, but he has killed lions and bears in that position, rescuing lambs right out of their mouths. David says, "The LORD who rescued me from the paw of the lion and the paw of the bear will rescue me from the hand of this Philistine" (v. 37).

Saul gives in. David can fight Goliath.

What happens next does little to reassure the Israelites. Saul lets David borrow his armor, but he's so laden down with it that he can't even walk.

Time to back out? Not David. He throws off the armor and chooses five smooth stones from the ravine. There's more than one way to kill a giant. Goliath may be a huge, hulking killing machine, but David has mobility on his side—and God.

Goliath, like David's brothers, resorts to mockery as he looks across at this unhelmeted, unarmored, unshielded shepherd carrying nothing but a shepherd's staff, a sling, and a few rocks in a bag. Goliath can't believe this kid, this pretty boy, so handsome and immature, is challenging him. Pitiful.

David is undaunted. He comes in the name of the Lord Almighty, the God of the armies of Israel. Not only does he plan to win, but also he promises to chop off the giant's head. "This very day I will give the carcasses of the Philistine army to the birds and the wild animals," David says, "and the whole world will know that there is a God in Israel. All those gathered here will know that it is not by sword or spear that the LORD saves; for the battle is the LORD's, and he will give all of you into our hands" (vv. 46-47).

Big words from such an overmatched challenger! The fight is on. David reaches into his bag, takes out a stone, slings it, and hits Goliath in his most vulnerable spot, his head. The stone sinks into his forehead, and the giant falls.

David had five stones, but he didn't need that many. One was plenty. As promised, he cuts off Goliath's head (with the giant's own sword) and gives it to the king. The Philistines flee, and the Israelites chase them down.

Slaughter of Goliath—a Story for Kids?

A story about a young man who kills someone by smashing his skull with a rock and decapitating him with a sword might sound like a questionable story to teach children, but it has been the subject of countless Sunday school lessons, dozens of children's books, and numerous animated and other kid-friendly films over the years. My own first memory of the story dates back to my very early childhood in Sunday school. Not only did our teacher narrate it, with the help of the felt-board story display so popular in that era, but we also sang a song about it, called "Only a Boy Named David." The song includes hand motions, especially when the sling goes "'round and 'round / And 'round and 'round" above your head. In the end, "the giant came / Tumbling down."[2]

One of the ways my own children learned the David and Goliath story was through the *Veggie Tales* film, mentioned earlier, "Dave and the Giant Pickle." I can't even count the number of times I watched it with them. As the name suggests, the characters in the *Veggie Tales* animated films are vegetables. The characters are funny and cute, their songs stick in your head way longer than you wish they would, and each story teaches a moral lesson. Bob the Tomato tells the story of Dave, a small asparagus, who takes on Goliath, the Giant Pickle. This retelling of the story focuses on Dave as the underdog. Not only is he smaller than Goliath, but even before the giant enters the story, Dave feels overshadowed by his older and bigger brothers. Even the sheep make Dave look small.

When Dave's father, Jesse, runs to tell his sons that the Philistines are about to attack, all the brothers laugh at Dave when he volunteers to go help fight to save Israel. They can't see Dave, with his short stature and high-pitched, little-boy voice, as anything but the brother they like to pick on. The brothers hurry to the front lines to fight, and Dave is left behind with the sheep. Jesse eventually sends Dave to the front, but only to bring food to the brothers.

Dave discovers that his brothers and the rest of the Israelite army have been scared into submission by Goliath. The giant, who is a huge but not very bright pickle, is so daunting that his stride makes the ground shake. He taunts his enemy with a booming voice, but no one will fight him. Dave steps up and defeats him with his sling and stones. What's the lesson? The Israelites had forgotten that even though the enemy is big, God is bigger. With God's help, Dave became a "really little guy who did a really big thing."[3]

Despite the killing and decapitation that are part of the David and Goliath story, dozens of children's authors have found the story ideal for their audience. The biblical text follows a pattern that is much easier than many other stories from Scripture to translate into an action-packed, plot-oriented story with a clear message. In many of these stories, David's youth is emphasized. He is a little boy, not the strong, good-looking young man that Michelangelo sculpted. One children's book I read even gives David a cute little dog who accompanies him as David plays his harp for the sheep. But the small boy also kills a lion with a rock.

None of these children's books spends much time developing the character of Goliath. He is simply a big bully. He mocks and intimidates. He must seem like a very familiar figure to the young readers who no doubt have encountered their own bully "giants" at school and elsewhere. What satisfaction it must give these young readers to identify with little David as he knocks this tormentor down.

Why Does David Win? He Brings a Rock to a Sword Fight

The David and Goliath story teaches children some things about self-esteem, the importance of relying on God, and the ways that the underdog can sometimes win over a bigger foe. But the story has been employed to illustrate some lessons for adults too. Malcolm Gladwell takes a psychological, self-help approach to the story in his popular book *David and Goliath: Underdogs, Misfits, and the Art of Battling Giants*. He believes it's a misreading of the story to think that David's victory over Goliath is miraculous or even all that unlikely if you look at what really happens. David wins against Goliath because he fights a different battle than what Goliath was expecting. David doesn't fight Goliath's strengths. He identifies and attacks his weaknesses. David may look scrawnier and less heavily armed, but in fact, he is simply a different kind of warrior. What if the greatest boxer in the world showed up to fight a ninety-eight-pound weakling? It might look like certain slaughter for the little guy. But what if that little guy pulled out a gun and shot the boxer? That's not fair according to the rules of boxing, but the underdog would walk away alive.

It's not that Goliath is a warrior and David isn't. It's that they are two different kinds of warriors, and David's strategy is smarter. David is a projectile warrior, a slinger, which was a recognized and important type of combatant in ancient warfare. Goliath is a heavy-infantry soldier. David doesn't have Goliath's multiple heavy weapons and massive protective armor, but he has mobility and speed. He also has a stone that, if properly propelled from the sling, could hit the giant's forehead with the force of a bullet from a fair-sized modern handgun.[4]

Why does Goliath tell David to come to him rather than rushing toward David himself? Why does Goliath refer to "sticks" when he asks about David's shepherd's staff? Why does he need a shield bearer to guide him out? Gladwell suggests Goliath may have a condition called acromegaly, a pituitary-gland tumor that might explain his extraordinary height and that might also cause him to have restricted sight and double vision. He sees two sticks when there is only one. He needs someone to guide him forward because he can't see where he's going. He misjudges David because he cannot see and assess his opponent clearly.[5] Goliath may be a giant, but he has significant weaknesses. David may look weak, but he has significant strengths. The more agile, more strategically adept man wins.

By looking at the stories of a wide range of people, Gladwell applies the lessons of this biblical story in a variety of ways to how people can fight the "giants" that face them in their own lives. What may appear to be a disadvantage to the giant-fighting person can sometimes be the very key to his or her real strength.

Renowned attorney David Boies, for example, struggled with dyslexia, even though for years he did not know that was what made reading so difficult for him. He didn't learn to read until third grade, and even then, he did so very slowly. He never learned to love reading. So how could he possibly succeed in the reading-heavy profession of the law? Just as David used a sling and stone instead of a javelin and sword, Boies used listening and memorizing to compensate for his lack of reading ability. He developed strong skills in both of those areas, which allowed him to catch things others missed and be able to present issues clearly and concisely to judges and jurors. He wishes he could read better, but his "giant" of a disability was slain by other strengths that made up for it.[6]

Michelangelo Carves David out of a Giant

Veggie Tales and children's books and Malcolm Gladwell retell and reinterpret the David and Goliath story, but some artists, writers, business owners, TV-show producers, and others use only a portion of the story to fit their purposes. They rely on the assumption that most people already know the basic story, so all they have to do is tap into it. If you were to ask many people across the world what image comes to mind when they think of the biblical David, they would picture Michelangelo's five-hundred-year-old statue, in which David holds a sling in his hand. Michelangelo's image of David may not be all that accurate as a portrait of the young shepherd described in the Bible—there would be no reason for the biblical David to be naked, for example—but the seventeen-foot-tall work of art does capture David's heroic quality. As the sculptor's biographer William E. Wallace puts it, the sculpture "is truthful to the spirit of David, who was a giant-slayer and future king, and whose faith and courage were of such gigantic proportions."[7]

Michelangelo's creation of that statue is in itself a kind of David versus Goliath story. Today, Michelangelo is so revered that it may seem hard to imagine that he ever had to struggle to establish himself as an artist, but before he sculpted *David*, he found himself needing to accomplish something big in order to not be overshadowed by a rival who would also go down in history as one of the greatest of all time. That artist was Leonardo da Vinci, who was working in Florence at the time that Michelangelo returned there after five years in Rome.

Besides this daunting competition, Michelangelo also had to contend with a block of marble that was not ideal. Considering the fact that he was about to sculpt the most famous giant slayer in history, it is ironic that the huge block of marble the artist had available to him was already known as the "Giant" even before he gained access to it. It was not a new block of marble, having been quarried more than forty years earlier. That lack of freshness makes the material harder to work with. Furthermore, three other artists had already tried to use it and had been defeated by this "Giant."

Like the character he was creating, Michelangelo succeeded marvelously, and his rendering of this biblical hero is better known than the countless others produced across the centuries. In Wallace's words, "For Florentines, David was an exemplar of strength and courage in the face of adversity and a hero with whom they closely identified. So too did Michelangelo identify with *David*—as David slew Goliath, so did the young Michelangelo conquer the giant block of marble."[8] The sculpture was given the best spot in Florence's main piazza, and the artist went on to gain many more commissions.

Many other artists have sensed the dramatic potential of the David and Goliath story and have depicted it in their work. In 1544, Titian painted a graphic and powerful painting of David praying beside the corpse of Goliath, whose decapitated head rests nearby. In 1607, Caravaggio followed a similar theme in his painting *David with the Head of Goliath*. Peter Paul Rubens's 1616 painting *David Slaying Goliath* shows a sword-wielding David hovering over the fallen Goliath. David's foot rests on the giant's head as the victor prepares to cut that head off. Dozens of other paintings and statues depicting this story could be listed, not to mention many other works of art that portray other elements of David's life.

Authors writing about every imaginable subject have tied their books to the David and Goliath theme. Andrew Soltis wrote *David vs. Goliath Chess: How to Beat a Strong Player*. Writing about the current Middle East politics, Joshua Muravchik published *Making David into Goliath: How the World Turned against Israel*. In the business realm, Matt Stoller wrote *Goliath: The 100-Year War between Monopoly Power and Democracy*, and Bruce Schneider published *Data and Goliath: The Hidden Battles to Collect Your Data and Control Your World*. Authors too numerous to mention have treated the David and Goliath theme psychologically and spiritually, showing how to defeat "Goliaths" in life, such as depression, procrastination, stress, perfectionism, resentment, addiction, fear, doubt, bad habits, failures, rejection, and anger.

One advertising agency so resonated with David's defeat of Goliath that they named their company David&Goliath (yes, one word). Like David, they say that they are "nimble enough to move and adapt" at the speed of the market and "brave enough to question the status quo rather than follow the lead of others." They say the company was "built on the simple idea that no challenge is too big, too small or too difficult."[9]

The reality TV show *Survivor* employed the David and Goliath personas to profile and select their cast for the 2018 season. As one of the show's producers told the *Hollywood Reporter*, "We started meeting people and realizing, 'Wow, people are either a David or a Goliath.' There are very few people who are both."[10] They began to label each person they interviewed as either a David or Goliath and eventually came up with ten of each to make up their new cast.

David Is a Hero—but That's Not All He Is

David is a hero in his confrontation with the giant. If that were the only story Scripture told about him, it would still be worth reading and retelling and filming and painting. But the biblical portrait of David is far more complex and conflicted. Some elements of his story may sound like something out of an action/adventure film, but the intensity of his heroism is matched elsewhere by the depth of his wicked deeds. Some may squirm to read about this less admirable—and at times even despicable—side of David. Some readers may even wonder whether such things should have been included in Scripture. Do they dilute David's heroism? How can I admire someone who was so good and yet also so bad?

I am grateful that the Bible includes such a nuanced portrait of David. Superheroes are easy to find in movies and comic books, but that's not what Scripture is offering. David is a flawed man. He fascinates not only because he could kill a giant but also because his passions and actions run the gamut of human behavior. He killed. He loved. He betrayed. He led. He danced. He agonized. He had problems with women, with his children, with sin, with his government, with God, with himself, and with life. He was misunderstood, abused, praised, rebuked, and chased. We have looked at David and Goliath, but we could also look at David and Jonathan, David and Saul, David and Absalom, David and Michal, David and Achish, David and Nabal, David and Abigail, and others. All those stories are included in Scripture, and each is worth contemplating.

Hardly a person exists who cannot relate to some portion of his story, and sometimes many portions of it. The Bible does not sanitize him. His story warns and inspires just as much through his flaws as through his strengths.

David and Bathsheba: The Hero Falls

Let's consider just one of those other David stories, the story of David and Bathsheba. Just as "David and Goliath" is one of the most famous hero stories in the world, "David and Bathsheba" is one of the most famous sex scandals in history. It contains the exalted tragedy of great literature and also the tawdriness of any run-of-the-mill celebrity scandal we might run across today. The story is as tragic and powerful as anything out of Greek drama or Shakespeare. It has murder, lust, shame, exposure, redemption, and consequences. David is at the center of the story, but he is about as far from the Goliath-slaying young shepherd as you can get.

This story starts the way many tragedies do—with the desire to possess something belonging to someone else. Like any tragic hero out of Shakespeare or Greek tragedy, David is blinded by power, pride, and lust. He takes Bathsheba because he can. He thinks he can get away with it, even though she is someone else's wife. He pays a heavy price, and so do those around him.

By the time this story begins, David is no longer an unknown young man with a sling and stones. Now he is the king. He is powerful, feared, and admired. He is used to getting what he wants. He can order people around. He has acknowledged God in the past. Now, other forces inside him have the upper hand.

The king, at home in Jerusalem while his men are off fighting, walks around on the roof of his house. He looks down and sees a woman bathing. She is beautiful.

You can already see what's coming, right? But what happens next is not inevitable. David has a decision to make. Men see beautiful women at a distance regularly, but that doesn't mean they act on that desire. Plenty of restraints hold them back—marriage, social customs, modesty. But David is the king. Although God and his people may hold him to a high standard, the power and influence over others that his position allows tempts him to act.

David takes the first step. He asks who the woman is. She is Bathsheba, daughter of Eliam, but even more significantly for this situation, she is the wife of Uriah the Hittite. Wife, married, unavailable—such is Bathsheba.

In my mind, because of all the retellings of this story that I have seen and heard in films, paintings, sermons, and elsewhere, the next part of the story takes a significant amount of time. But in Scripture, it takes up only two devastating verses: "Then David sent messengers to get her. She came to him, and he slept with her. (Now she was purifying herself from her monthly uncleanness.) Then she went back home. The woman conceived and sent word to David, saying, 'I am pregnant'" (2 Samuel 11:4-5).

So much is crammed into those few words! The disaster looms. But much is left out also. What was Bathsheba's attitude toward this summons? Did she have the power to say no even if she wanted to? Keep in mind, this relationship is not between two people of equal status. This is not like a modern affair between two neighbors or two coworkers who suddenly find themselves attracted to each other and fall to temptation. This incident happens in a time and culture in which someone with *all* the power—David the *man* and David the *king*—summons someone to him who has *no* power—Bathsheba the *woman* and Bathsheba the *subject*. She has no choice but to do what he says. We don't get the details about Bathsheba's feelings about these actions of the king, and David's thoughts are not presented here either. What did he say to her? How did he rationalize this to himself? So much is left unknown. The story hurries on.

The next verse begins the cover-up, so familiar to us in our scandal-plagued day. David hatches a plan that looks foolproof. He calls Uriah back from battle, meets with him, and tells him to go home and "wash your feet," a euphemism for sexual intercourse. If Uriah does so, that will give a plausible explanation for Bathsheba's pregnancy, scandal will be avoided, and all will be well.

Uriah refuses to play along. He doesn't go down to his house. David's servants tell him that Uriah spent the night at the entrance of the king's house instead. David confronts Uriah to ask why. Uriah's response makes David's guilt look even worse. Uriah says that while his fellow soldiers are camping in the open fields, "How could I go to my house to eat and drink and make love to my wife? As surely as you live, I will not do such a thing!" (v. 11).

The more David tries to cover up, the more desperate he becomes. He doubles down on evil. He writes a letter to Joab, Uriah's commander—a letter Uriah himself must deliver—that orders Joab to put Uriah at the forefront of battle so he will be killed. The ploy works. Uriah is killed. Bathsheba mourns, but as soon as the time of mourning ends, David brings her to his house and makes her his wife.

That may sound like the end of the story, and David no doubt hoped it was. After all, who would have the nerve to confront him? The final sentence of chapter 11 answers that question: "But the thing David had done displeased the LORD" (v. 27).

David may be able to manipulate everyone else, but the Lord has other plans. He sends Nathan to confront David, not directly, but in a way that would be even more powerful, a way that would wake up David to his own sin. Nathan tells a parable, using the story in much the same way that Jesus would use his own parables to teach and challenge his listeners generations later. The value of a parable is that the listener can consider it without knowing that it's about *him*. David's defenses are down. Nathan tells of a rich man and a poor man. The rich man has many flocks and herds, but the poor man has only one lamb, so precious to him that it is almost like a member of the family. When a traveler comes, the rich man ignores his own vast flock and instead takes the poor man's lamb to feed the guest.

David is outraged by this story. The man who did that should die! He should pay the poor man fourfold what he took from him.

Then, in one of the most dramatic moments of the story, Nathan responds, "You are the man!" (12:7).

Nathan goes on to deliver the Lord's message to David. He reminds David of all the Lord had done for him in rescuing him from Saul and establishing him as king of Judah and Israel. And now David has done evil in the Lord's sight. He will pay a heavy price, part of which will be paid soon, such as the death of the child, and part of which will unfold over time, such as the rebellion of his sons and other turmoil in his kingdom.

Having heard this devastating prophecy, David has a choice. Will he continue to try to cover up and manage the crisis, to make excuses and wiggle out of responsibility for what he has done?

David responds, "I have sinned against the LORD" (v. 13). No more dodging responsibility. No more power plays. David confesses.

"The LORD has taken away your sin," responds Nathan (v. 13). David is forgiven. He will not die. But neither will he escape the consequences of his sin.

What Was David *Thinking* during the Bathsheba Scandal?
Psalm 51

The David and Bathsheba story is packed with drama and action, but as is so common in biblical narratives, it doesn't slow down to tell us much about the thoughts and feelings of the people involved. Did David feel guilty for what he was doing? What was going through his mind as he handed Uriah the message that would lead to the soldier's death? How did Bathsheba feel about the death of her husband? How aware was she of what David was plotting?

One thing that sets David apart from many other figures in the Bible is that we have psalms to serve as commentary on many of the events of his life. Those psalms delve deeply into David's feelings, which run the gamut from joy to anger to fear to guilt to hope. The superscription on Psalm 51 says, "A psalm of David. When the prophet Nathan came to him after David had committed adultery with Bathsheba." David's attitude in this psalm is one of sorrow, repentance, and a cry for mercy:

Have mercy on me, O God,
according to your unfailing love;
according to your great compassion
blot out my transgressions.
Wash away all my iniquity
and cleanse me from my sin. (Vv. 1-2)

Gone is the arrogant king who took another man's wife just because he had the power to do so. Gone is the master manipulator who sent that husband to his death in a way that David hoped would cover his own tracks. The David in this psalm is intensely aware of his sin, and he also trusts in God's love and mercy to forgive him. He confesses his sin, but he doesn't wallow in it. He writes as someone beloved of God, someone God wants to restore:

Create in me a pure heart, O God,
and renew a steadfast spirit within me.
Do not cast me from your presence
or take your Holy Spirit from me.
Restore to me the joy of your salvation
and grant me a willing spirit, to sustain me. (Vv. 10-12)

Retelling the Irresistible Story

The story of David and Bathsheba has fascinated artists, filmmakers, and writers just as much as the David and Goliath story. McKenzie writes, "Truth be told, these faults of David's attract our attention more than his virtues. We admire the fearless and pious young hero, but we cannot identify with him. The adulterer who gets caught in a cover-up, on the other hand, is one of us."[11]

Although the story provides a complex story of David, Bathsheba has been the focus for many artists. She is one of the most frequently painted women of the Bible, and painters have offered their own interpretations of this enigmatic woman for hundreds of years. Cezanne, Peter Paul Rubens, Jan Steen, Willem Drost, and countless other painters have portrayed Bathsheba. Rembrandt's *Bathsheba at Her Bath* is one of the most famous of these works, finished in 1654 and now hanging in the Louvre. Bathsheba is nude, and she sits on white sheets as a servant washes her feet. Bathsheba holds a paper loosely in her hand, presumably the summons from King David. Her expression is one of the most intriguing aspects of the painting. She looks downward, her face full of sadness, and perhaps resignation, as if filled with a foreboding of all the tragedy that is about to unfold because of what is written on that little piece of paper.

The Bible is mysterious about Bathsheba's feelings and motives, but filmmakers who take on this story do not have the option of silence on those issues. They have to show Bathsheba speaking and taking action, so they have no choice but to interpret her behavior. One of the most popular movie versions of the story is the 1951 film *David and Bathsheba*, starring Gregory Peck and Susan Hayward. In this film, the unequal power dynamics between Bathsheba and David are played down. The story comes across more as a 1950s love affair than it does as the exploitation of Bathsheba that it was. In this version, Bathsheba is portrayed as very much complicit in the affair that leads to the death of her husband. When she is summoned to David after he sees her bathing naked (behind a screen), she at first acts as if she has no choice but to give in to his wishes. He is the king, and she must do what he says.

David tells her he does not want to take her by force. When he is about to send her away, she reveals that she spoke as she did only because she wanted to know what was in his heart. She has been watching him. She knew he would be home and that he would see her bathing, so that's why she was out there. There is no love in her marriage. Her marriage was arranged, and she didn't meet Uriah until the day of their wedding. She wants to be David's wife, but she is not free. The action that follows removes that marital barrier—with huge consequences.[12]

The Appeal of David—It's Personal

David has a commanding presence not only in the Old Testament but throughout the New Testament as well. When the angel comes and tells Mary that she will conceive a child from the Holy Spirit and will name him Jesus, he emphasizes the importance of the ancestry of David. The angel says about Jesus, "He will be great and will be called the Son of the Most High. The Lord God will give him the throne of his father David, and he will reign over Jacob's descendants forever; his kingdom will never end" (Luke 1:32-33). Jesus himself talks about David, and so does Paul. David is a crucial figure in Christianity.

Christians love David not only because of his importance in the overarching story of the Bible but also because they can relate to him so readily. In the stories I have examined in this chapter, it's hard to resist responding to them not just from a distant, theological, or historical perspective but also for what they teach about life.

The story of David's battle with Goliath gives hope because it turns the usual expectations about power upside down. Everyone is afraid of Goliath because he is huge, covered with armor, and wields multiple death-dealing weapons. The story reveals that those aren't the only forces that matter. David is agile, smart, and well equipped with the weapons that suit *him*. He doesn't try to win by being Goliath. He wins by being David and by walking in the power God gives him. I learn from David not to compare myself to others. I may not be the giant, but I don't need to be. I follow the Lord's lead. A spiritual dynamic is at work in this story that is the opposite of the usual worldly values: the last will be first. Jesus, in his own way, would later emphasize in his teaching this theme, as well as the others found in this story.

The David and Bathsheba story is filled with tragedy, but ultimately it also offers readers hope. David does horrible things, but his repentance and God's forgiveness also show that no sin puts any of us so far from God that we are unforgivable. God restores. He responds to repentance. From

Psalm 51 I learn from David to pray, "Create in me a pure heart, O God" (v. 10), and "Hide your face from my sins and blot out all my iniquity" (v. 9). David is one of the greatest kings in biblical history and is referred to as "a man after [God's] own heart" (1 Samuel 13:14), yet he fell. But that moral failure was not the final word.

Anyone who questions the continued relevance of the Old Testament needs to go no further than the story of David to see its timeless appeal. I have only scratched the surface of the artists, filmmakers, and other purveyors of pop culture who have drawn from David. Writers cannot resist him. Dip into almost any era of literature over the centuries, and you'll find David. What about twentieth-century American fiction? David is there in novels such as Sherwood Anderson's *Winesburg, Ohio* and William Faulkner's *Absalom, Absalom!* What about sixteenth-century British literature? David is there in Edmund Spenser's *The Faerie Queene*. In their book on the influence of the David story on Western literature, Raymond-Jean Frontain and Jan Wojcik found David treated in the works of writers as varied as George Peele, Antoine de Montchrestien, Hans Sachs, Tirso de Molina, John Dryden, Christopher Smart, Michael Drayton, Robert Aylett, Jacques de Coras, Thomas Fuller, Thomas Lodge, D. H. Lawrence, André Gide, Theodore Roethke, and Yehuda Amichai.[13]

One of the things I love most about the David story is that I can never simply settle it in my mind and then move on to something else. The life of this man, with the many unexpected turns and incidents, keeps playing itself out in my mind, as I linger in its ambiguities and find nuances that had eluded me before. No wonder this story plays such a commanding role in the biblical narrative.

Notes

1. Steven L. McKenzie, *King David: A Biography* (Oxford, UK: Oxford University Press, 2000), 2.

2. Arthur Arnott, "Only a Boy Named David," © 1931 Salvationist Publishing and Supplies Ltd., CCLI Song No. 72013, Music Services, https://musicservices.org/license/song/detail/125138.

3. Phil Vischer, writer and director, *Veggie Tales*, episode 5, "Dave and the Giant Pickle" (Chicago: Big Idea Productions, 1996; Burbank, CA: Warner Home Video, 2004), DVD.

4. Malcolm Gladwell, *David and Goliath: Underdogs, Misfits, and the Art of Battling Giants* (New York: Little, Brown, 2013), 11.

5. Gladwell, 13-15.

6. Gladwell, 107-10.

7. William E. Wallace, *Michelangelo: The Artist, the Man, and His Times* (New York: Cambridge University Press, 2010), 61.

8. Wallace, 61.

9. "About," David&Goliath (website), accessed April 14, 2021, http://dng-com.herokuapp.com/about.

10. Josh Wigler, "'Survivor: David vs. Goliath': Jeff Probst Reveals Everything to Know about Season 37," *Hollywood Reporter*, September 5, 2018, https://www.hollywoodreporter.com/live-feed/survivor-david-goliath-jeff-probst-season-37-1139268.

11. McKenzie, *King David: A Biography*, 154.

12. *David and Bathsheba*, directed by Henry King (1951; Beverly Hills, CA: Twentieth Century Fox Home Entertainment, 2013), DVD.

13. Raymond-Jean Frontain and Jan Wojcik, eds., introduction to *The David Myth in Western Literature* (West Lafayette, IN: Purdue University Press, 1980).

Digging Deeper

1. Why is the story of David and Goliath so popular with children? Is it simply a matter of the little guy defeating the big bully, or are there other spiritual lessons kids might learn from this story? Is the violence of the story—smashing a man's skull with a rock and then cutting off his head—problematic when presenting it to children?

2. This chapter says, "David is a flawed man. He fascinates not only because he could kill a giant but also because his passions and actions run the gamut of human behavior. He killed. He loved. He betrayed. He led. He danced. He agonized. He had problems with women, with his children, with sin, with his government, with God, with himself, and with life. He was misunderstood, abused, praised, rebuked, and chased." When you think of David, what stories stand out to you? Even though he is a complex man who could be described in many ways, both good and bad, how would you describe his legacy?

3. In the David and Bathsheba story, what is at the core of David's sin? Lust? Pride? An obsession with power? Self-centeredness? Why does Nathan's parable work better than a direct accusation to confront David with his sin?

4. Do you have any situations in your life right now in which you feel like the young David, with odds stacked against you by some Goliath-sized difficulty? Does this story offer hope or a fresh perspective?

Go to https://www.thefoundrypublishing.com/8OT/LeaderGuide for a free downloadable leader's guide that includes more questions for reflection as well as activities for use in a small group setting.

3

Expulsion from Paradise // Francesco Curradi // c. 1570–1661

Eve and Adam—
Paradise, Sin, Cover-Up

[1] *Now the serpent was more crafty than any of the wild animals the* LORD *God had made. He said to the woman, "Did God really say, 'You must not eat from any tree in the garden'?"*

[2] *The woman said to the serpent, "We may eat fruit from the trees in the garden,* [3] *but God did say, 'You must not eat fruit from the tree that is in the middle of the garden, and you must not touch it, or you will die.'"*

[4] *"You will not certainly die," the serpent said to the woman.* [5] *"For God knows that when you eat from it your eyes will be opened, and you will be like God, knowing good and evil."*

[6] *When the woman saw that the fruit of the tree was good for food and pleasing to the eye, and also desirable for gaining wisdom, she took some and ate it. She also gave some to her husband, who was with her, and he ate it.* [7] *Then the eyes of both of them were opened, and they realized they were naked; so they sewed fig leaves together and made coverings for themselves.*

—Genesis 3:1-7

ALMOST EVERYONE knows the story of Adam and Eve, but probably more people know it through parodies than know it from reading the story in Genesis. When I hear "Adam and Eve," the first thing my mind goes to are a whole slew of TV commercials, magazine ads, and memes that feature takeoffs on the story. Even as I write this chapter, the Cable News Network (CNN) is running a commercial in which bananas are placed where you would normally see apples, such as a student placing a banana on a teacher's desk and someone putting up a sign that says a banana a day keeps the doctor away. So of course they show Adam and Eve in a painting, with a banana replacing the supposed apple of the story.

Ironically, the point of the commercial is that if you tell something that is false long enough, people will begin to believe it. The implication is that news networks other than CNN falsely claim that things are bananas when they are really apples. And those networks repeat those banana lies so often that their viewers eventually go along with it. It's ironic because believing the forbidden fruit in the Adam and Eve story is an apple is just as false as believing it is a banana.

Countless renowned artists, such as Michelangelo, Rubens, and Klimt, have painted the Adam and Eve story over the centuries, but the story is so stark and well known that even an artist with the most limited skills could paint or draw it in a way that would still be recognizable. I could easily draw it on a napkin so that anyone would be able to identify it. A stick figure of a man standing next to a stick figure of a woman who is holding an apple might be enough. If I wanted to get fancy, I could add some fig leaves covering the relevant places. Add a slithery serpent and a tree or two and I'm done.

Some professional artists have simplified their representations of the story even further. Hiroko Sakai's painting *Adam's Dilemma* shows two hands holding an apple-like fruit. Ana Maria Edulescu's *Original Sin* features two partial close-up views of an apple, each with a bite taken out of it, and, in one of the views, a little green leaf at the top of the apple. The Fine Art America website, which offers 468 different Adam and Eve paintings for sale, also offers the *Original Sin* print on various products, including beach towels, tote bags, greeting cards, and spiral notebooks.[1]

Nicolae Gutu's *Eve* shows a woman with what looks like a human hand covering her eyes, but with serpent scales further down the arm. In her hand, she holds an apple. Karen Jane Jones's *Temptation 2* shows a serpent wrapped around an apple that has one bite taken out of it. Those are only a few of the variations on the Adam and Eve theme. Viewers don't need to be *told* the story so much as they simply need to be *reminded* of it. Everybody knows it already.

Or at least people think they know it. The way most people picture the story is almost never purely biblical, mixed as it is with so many countless retellings and cartoons and paintings and images. Think of the story right now as you have always pictured it. You know it, right? About what age do Adam and Eve appear to be? What do you base that on? What is their skin color? Are they light skinned with brown hair? Or are they dark skinned with black hair? Based on what evidence? And how about the serpent? What does he look like? What about that fruit? Is it an apple? Maybe, contrary to the CNN commercial, it really did look more like a banana. Or a pear or a watermelon or a kumquat or some fruit that no one has ever seen. How about the garden of Eden? Is it junglelike, with huge trees and ferns and flowers? Or is it tamer, with meadows and streams?

These questions are not answered in the biblical text. We fill them in, or rather, we think we already known them and have always known them, for who can really remember a time when you didn't already know the story? One reason people have so readily filled in the gaps with their own details is that the story, while huge in its impact, is brief in the telling. In Genesis, the entire story, from the first mention of God placing Adam in Eden to the banishment of Adam and Eve from the garden, takes up a mere forty-one verses. That momentous passage in Genesis 2 and 3 includes the creation of Eve, the temptation by the serpent, the eating of the forbidden fruit, and the curses that followed. With so much story in so little space, details are understandably sparse.

That leaves room for people to use the story as they see fit. And it's easy to see why so many want to use it for their own purposes. The Adam and Eve story has everything: high stakes, forbidden desire, sex, suspense, deception, tragedy, and dramatic action. Advertisers love it for all those reasons, but they generally value it for a message that is exactly the opposite of the story's purpose in Genesis. The fall, as the sin of Adam and Eve is often called, was not only the great tragedy in the lives of these two individuals but also the fall of humanity, the ushering in of sin and its consequences into human life, and the fall of creation itself. It is a disaster from which the whole world is still reeling. Christians see the fall as the reason Jesus Christ had to come to rescue us.

The Serpent as Triumphant Salesperson

But for advertisers, the surrender to sin was something else entirely. It was a triumph of sales skill. It was about getting people to give in to a temptation and pay whatever cost was necessary to acquire what the salesperson was offering. Far from being tragic, it's a success! From that perspective, the serpent is not Satan. Instead, he is the ultimate successful marketer. As Linda S. Schearing and Valarie H. Ziegler put it in their book *Enticed by Eden*, the serpent "promotes an action (the eating of the fruit) in its best possible light. He emphasizes the advantage of eating while minimizing any of its undesirable effects. In fact, what the snake does sounds a lot like a good marketing campaign."[2]

In this marketing approach toward the story, Eve's acquiescence to the serpent's temptation is seen not as a moral failure but as a daring, admirable choice. Dozens of print ads and TV commercials have exploited that theme. In the 1970s, ads for Eve cigarettes featured the slogan "There's a little Eve in every woman." The packages featured a painting of a colorful flower garden. In the midst of it, visible only from the neck up, a beautiful young woman gazes forward, flowers in her hair. The filter tips of the ciga-rette, visible in some of the ads, are covered in the floral pattern. Some ads show women dressed in clothing with the same floral pattern that appears on the cigarette box. Related products were also available. One Eve ad of-fered an Eve bag and belt embroidery kit. The kit allowed the consumer to embroider a pattern of apples onto a bag or belt. The ad says, "The nicest thing about our pretty apples is they aren't quite like any other. But neither is our Eve cigarette. It is as flavorful as it is pretty."[3]

Beauty is an ongoing theme of the Eve cigarette ads. One of the slogans used in many of them says, "Farewell to the ugly cigarette. Smoke pretty. Eve." No tragedy here. No sin. No terrible consequences. The "apple" is not a symbol of moral failure. It's pretty! Smoking is pretty! Sure, Eve gave into temptation to eat the apple, but who cares? It looks nice when you embroider it on a bag. Eve was bold, daring. She wanted something and took it. Why not? There is a little Eve in every woman. If you are a woman, there is some Eve in you, so embrace her. If you want to smoke, go ahead! You'll be more beautiful if you do.

Many advertisers who use the Adam and Eve theme enhance the for-bidden or "naughty" quality of whatever product they are selling. An air of scandal or taboo surrounding a product makes it even more appeal-ing. A Smirnoff commercial shows a modern, well-dressed Adam and Eve cautiously stepping out of an elevator and heading toward the door of a ballroom in a fancy hotel. At one point they stop in the hallway, and the camera angle makes it look as if the leaves of the potted plants are fig leaves covering them in strategic places. As they approach the double doors, an eye is shown looking out from a peephole, as if they are about to enter a forbidden place.

They enter a ballroom filled with attractive people wearing dresses and suits. A couple is shown enjoying a passionate kiss. Adam and Eve head toward the bar. A bartender sets two empty glasses in front of them. Ser-pents crawl out of the bartender's sleeves and from the front of his shirt. Eve's expression is wide eyed, enthralled. A man in the party overturns a table. The serpents crack two big chunks of ice with their mouths and drop them into the glasses. The Smirnoff is poured into the glasses. A serpent squeezes an apple and lets the juice pour into the glasses. The serpents drop apple slices into the finished drinks. Adam and Eve sit at one of the tables and enjoy their drinks, as another couple dressed just like them enters the room.[4]

In these "forbidden fruit" Adam and Eve commercials, falling to temptation is always a good thing. Consuming the product leaves Adam and Eve happy, fulfilled, or somehow more satisfied, just as the serpent in the Genesis Adam and Eve story said they would be. The tragic aftermath of the sinful choice that appears in Genesis 3 is never shown in advertising. The commercials stop at the point of pleasure.

Humor is often a key element of Adam and Eve commercials. Doritos has sponsored a number of Crash the Super Bowl advertising contests in which people submit videos that could be used as thirty-second Doritos commercials. Many have used humorous Adam and Eve themes. In one, for example, Eve is shown walking through the garden, past a hissing snake, and then she reaches up toward an apple hanging from a tree. Dramatic music plays as she slowly lowers the apple toward her mouth. A scowling Adam is briefly shown, as Eve bites into the apple. She offers the apple to Adam, but he frowns, pulls out a bag of Doritos, and says "Nah, I'm good," and then he bites into a chip.[5]

In one sense, all this may sound like harmless fun. After all, these ads aren't *replacing* the biblical Adam and Eve story. It's still right there in Genesis. Maybe the ads might even prompt someone to look it up in the Bible and see what it really says. Treating it humorously might even be considered a way of paying homage to the story. However, as Schearing and Ziegler point out in their book on how Western culture treats the Adam and Eve story, humor often has a serious purpose. Social media and other internet forms of humor are rife with Adam and Eve jokes, memes, and other content. Much of it has to do with relationships between men and women. The jokes these scholars analyze sometimes challenge gender stereotypes and sometimes propagate them. Humor about Adam and Eve "not only reflects society's attitudes and assumptions about gendered relationships (whether they focus on women, men, or both), but can also work to challenge and change them. On one level, jokes about Adam/man and Eve/woman not only comment on relationships, but also reflect the conflicts that exist between men and women in contemporary society."[6]

Sometimes the Adam and Eve jokes rely on sexist stereotypes about women—that they are overly emotional, that they are nagging, that they are mainly sex objects, and so on. One joke, for example, states that God created man and then rested. Then he created woman. The punch line is, "Since then, neither God nor man has rested. Amen."[7] Other jokes make Adam, and men in general, the target. These jokes also rely on stereotypes. Schearing and Ziegler analyze a joke list of the top ten reasons why God created Eve. They include reasons such as "God was worried that Adam would frequently become lost because he would not ask for directions" and "God knew that one day Adam would require someone to locate and hand him the remote."[8] These jokes are not vicious, and perhaps they are merely harmless bits of humor that acknowledge the complicated relationships between men and women. But like the Adam and Eve advertising, they might also trivialize the story over time, making the biblical account merely fodder for cheap shots and sexist thinking.

After all the jokes, ads, memes, and cartoons, can Adam and Eve be taken seriously anymore? For those who believe what this story teaches, the stakes in these chapters of Genesis are huge: the fall of humanity, the beginning of sin's consequences that still plague us today, and the desperate need for a savior. This story stays with us so vividly because, despite how it has been twisted and exploited, it still speaks across the centuries about what it means to be tempted, to fall to sin, and to lose Paradise. The biblical story, told with such precision in Genesis 3, contains something in every sentence, almost every phrase, that strikes a deep truth within us. Let us consider what it says.

A Man, a Woman, a Garden, a Serpent, a Tree

Genesis 1 tells of God creating "the heavens and the earth" (v. 1), but Genesis 2 focuses more intimately on the garden of Eden and its residents. Genesis 1 is on a grand scale. Genesis 2 gets personal. God "formed a man from the dust of the ground and breathed into his nostrils the breath of life, and the man became a living being" (2:7). God had already prepared a garden within Eden, where he placed the man to live. What was that garden like?

You have probably seen the paintings and other depictions of the garden of Eden. It is shown as a lush, green paradise, filled with trees, plants, colorful birds, waterfalls, and flowing streams. The Bible is achingly brief in its description of that garden. Some rivers are named, and we are told that God "made all kinds of trees grow out of the ground—trees that were pleasing to the eye and good for food" (v. 9). Two of those trees are named—the Tree of Life and the Tree of the Knowledge of Good and Evil. We also know that the garden contains birds, wild animals, and livestock, because God assigns Adam to name them. As far as a physical description of the place goes, that's about it. The rest is left to our imagination.

Adam was given not only a beautiful place to live but also work to do. Some have incorrectly believed that work itself was one of the punishments that sprang from the fall, but work was not a punishment. It was an activity that fit well into a life in Paradise. The fall later caused the ground to be cursed. Thorns and thistles grew, and work turned into sweaty and painful toil, but before that, Adam was given a meaningful and presumably enjoyable activity in his tending of the plants and animals of the garden.

Adam was now in a perfect place made specifically for him, surrounded by beauty, with plenty to do. He was naked and free. His conscience was clear. His future was bright. God placed only one restriction on him, but it didn't seem too burdensome: "You are free to eat from any tree in the garden; but you must not eat from the tree of the knowledge of good and evil, for when you eat from it you will certainly die" (vv. 16-17).

At this point in the story, Adam offers no objection to God's prohibition against eating from that tree. No response at all is recorded. What did he think of it? Did he ask why? Did his curiosity lead him to push the limits as far as he could without disobeying, maybe touching the tree or sniffing the fruit without eating it?

Or did he trust God so much that he was unconcerned about that tree? After all, there were plenty of other trees to choose from. For now, Adam was about to be hit with a new reality in his life that must have knocked trees and fruits far from the forefront of his thinking. He was about to get married! That's a big change for anyone, but it was especially significant for Adam, since women did not exist yet. God declares, "It is not good for the man to be alone. I will make a helper suitable for him" (v. 18).

"Helper." There's plenty of room for trouble and controversy in that English word, a rough translation of the Hebrew. As biblical commentator Joseph Coleson explains, a more precise translation of Genesis 2:18 would be, "I will make for him a power/strength corresponding/equal to him." Elaborating on that translation, Coleson writes that the Hebrew phrase

ʿēzer kěnegdô, which has often been translated as "helper to him" or something similar, in Hebrew means something closer to "a power/strength like him, corresponding to him, of the same kind or species, facing [or opposite] him as [an] equal." Understood in that way, the text "affirms the equality and mutuality of the genders—male and female, female and male. This theological (and anthropological) principle is crucial to understanding ourselves as created in the image of God."[9]

You might expect that immediately after God declared Adam's need for this companion, God would create one. Instead, God brings the various animals to Adam for him to name. This is followed by the statement, "But for Adam no suitable helper was found" (v. 20). God knew all along that none of the animals, as amazing as these creations were, would be suitable for Adam. But perhaps Adam needed to see that for himself. Maybe he felt a lack, a need for completion, but thought it could somehow be fulfilled by something else already in Paradise. He would naturally turn first to what existed, and a "woman" did not yet exist. He must have had trouble even imagining what one would be. But he knew he needed *something,* someone. He knew he was incomplete. He trusted God to create the someone he needed.

God did not simply make another human being who was similar to Adam, which he easily could have done. Instead, he created the woman from part of Adam's own body. That's how united they would be. God put Adam into a deep slumber, took a rib from his side, and then closed up Adam's wound. From that part of Adam, he created the new person, Eve.

"This is now bone of my bones and flesh of my flesh," said Adam, in his first recorded words. The following verses say, "That is why a man leaves his father and mother and is united to his wife, and they become one flesh. Adam and his wife were both naked, and they felt no shame" (vv. 23-25).

United. Feeling no shame. With God's creative act, two persons have become one. Even though so much of the discussion of the Adam and Eve story understandably focuses on the sin the two are about to commit, which has such devastating consequences on all of humanity, we shouldn't miss the beauty of this scene. It is the first marriage, the first blending of two people, the first relationship between human beings. Imagine what reality would be like if God had not set the world up this way. What if Adam had been allowed to simply live alone indefinitely at the top of God's creation, overseeing animals and plant life but having no one at his own level with whom to connect? What if God had created other humans only as separate entities incapable of the kind of intimacy that Adam and Eve shared? When you think of a world devoid of intimate relationships, it's easy to see why God said, "It is not good for the man to be alone" (v. 18). The Adam and Eve story has tragic elements, but it also contains world-changing beauty. If only we could stop the story there! But the tragedy is still to unfold.

The Adam and Eve story plays big in my mind, but in fact it is very short. God creates Eve in Genesis 2:22, and only four verses later, the serpent is already tempting her to eat. My mind reels with questions. How much time passed between Eve's creation and the appearance of the tempting serpent? What was Eve like? What was her relationship with Adam like in the time before that turn of events? How did they spend their days? What was it like to live in Eden? We only get one sentence about their marriage—they were naked and felt no shame. I want more details!

No one can definitively fill in what Genesis does not provide, although poets such as John Milton in *Paradise Lost* and artists in other creative fields used their imaginations to bring to life aspects of the story about which the Bible only hints. I do think it is useful not to jump too quickly from Eve's creation to her temptation. Because the story is so compressed in Scripture, it's easy to read it as if Eve was created on one day and then ate the forbidden fruit on the next, or maybe even created in the morning and then sinned in the afternoon.

But Genesis does not say how much time elapsed between Eve's creation and the appearance of the serpent. Could it have been several months? A year? A few years? Maybe a few decades? In that prefallen era, would they even have perceived time the way we do now?

Why spend time imagining all this? As a Christian, I believe this glimpse into the garden of Eden is a foreshadowing of what eternity will be like, just as certain passages in Revelation offer hints of that coming reality:

> Then I saw "a new heaven and a new earth," for the first heaven and the first earth had passed away, and there was no longer any sea. I saw the Holy City, the new Jerusalem, coming down out of heaven from God, prepared as a bride beautifully dressed for her husband. And I heard a loud voice from the throne saying, "Look! God's dwelling place is now among the people, and he will dwell with them. They will be his peo-

ple, and God himself will be with them and be their God. "He will wipe every tear from their eyes. There will be no more death" or mourning or crying or pain, for the old order of things has passed away." (21:1-4) That beautiful future is worth dwelling on as we now live in a fallen world that falls so short of it. God created the world in perfection and will return it to that state one day. Adam and Eve lived in it. They walked with God in the garden. They knew perfect beauty—in nature, in a relationship with each other, in a relationship with their Creator. They enjoyed meaningful work and lived in harmony with the animals, trees, streams, and other aspects of nature.

Today we live in a fallen world, but it is not so utterly fallen that all vestiges of that original beauty have been wiped away. Most of us have known moments of supreme contentment in beautiful gardens or beaches or mountains or meadows that we have visited. We have known moments when God's presence felt so close that we knew his Holy Spirit was right there with us. These intense times of joy make us ache for eternity with him. Adam and Eve did not have to ache for it. They did not have to hold on to tiny glimpses of eternity in a difficult world. Those glimpses were their entire reality. They lived that contentment every minute.

That is what makes their fall even more heartbreaking. Far from being a funny little joke in a thirty-second TV commercial, what happened in that garden was an enormous catastrophe from which the world has not yet been restored.

Along Came the Serpent

Genesis 3:1 begins, "Now the serpent was more crafty than any of the wild animals the LORD God had made." Into the ideal lives of Adam and Eve, this disruptive figure now has been inserted. Who is this serpent? We often speak of him as Satan, but Genesis 3 does not tell who he is or what he looks like or why he is there. Is it Satan appearing in the form of a serpent?

What we do know is that the serpent is crafty. This chapter not only narrates the fall of humanity but also gives a description of temptation that is still devastatingly relevant today—crafty. Temptation won't come in a form we can easily swat away; otherwise, it wouldn't be tempting. Wrongdoing tempts us when we can rationalize the behavior we are tempted to do. With certain behaviors we get so good at rationalizing them that we eventually really believe that evil is good.

We can probably identify that in ourselves, but it's even easier to see it in other people. We see a behavior others are doing or thinking about doing, and the destructiveness or wrongness of it cries out to us. Maybe it will lead to destroyed relationships, psychological or spiritual harm, financial ruin, or degradation and guilt. We think, *Don't do it! Flee the temptation! Stop! Repent!* Maybe we even tell them those things. Sometimes we can wake them up and get them to turn around, but at other times, we watch helplessly as they take the plunge into harmful activity. We wonder why they can't see the stupidity of this.

The serpent is crafty. All of us have been fighting the crafty tempter our whole lives. Adam and Eve had not. They lived in Paradise. They had never sinned. They had never seen someone sin. They had never faced the painful consequences of immorality, nor had they seen anyone else face those consequences. The serpent approached.

He starts with a question: "Did God really say, 'You must not eat from any tree in the garden'?" (Genesis 3:1).

"Did God really say, . . . ?" Notice the purpose of those first words. How much of our own rationalization follows that same pattern? To rationalize a wrong behavior, the first step is to create doubt about its wrongness. Did God really say we can't do that? Is it really wrong? Does God really care about that? Does God even speak to issues like that? Does God speak at all? Does God even exist? Why should I follow rules made up by someone else? Why can't I do what I want and use my own judgment?

God had been very clear: *You may not eat from that one tree.* There is no wiggle room in his statement, no gray area, no confusing part that is open to interpretation. So how can the serpent persuade Eve to disobey? He creates doubt in what she really heard. Did God really say it? Maybe she heard wrong. Maybe she misunderstood. The serpent starts off slowly, making her question herself and her own understanding. It is important to note that although only Eve is mentioned at this point in the conversation, the grammar indicates that Adam was right there with her. According to Coleson, the serpent uses the *plural* verb form for "you may not eat." Coleson adds, "Thus, the report that the serpent spoke 'to the woman' may reflect only that the woman answered, while the man did not."[10]

The serpent also deliberately falsifies and exaggerates what God had said. Did God really say they could not eat from *any* tree in the garden? Temptation rarely comes at us in a straightforward manner, with accurately stated facts. What the serpent is asking sort of sounds true. At first, if we're not paying close attention, we might even think it is true, but the serpent's first words are not simply an honest question. They are a way of presenting a lie. God didn't say they couldn't eat from any tree, but if the serpent can engage Eve in a conversation about the limits, and can get her to doubt or second-guess what those limits are, then he has already gone part of the way toward persuading her to question everything about what God has said.

The serpent exaggerates in his question, and Eve exaggerates in her answer. That's how temptation works. If you're going to step away from the truth to rationalize a behavior, your conscience will accept it more easily if you take baby steps away from the truth rather than start with an outright lie.

Eve easily could have told the serpent what God's restriction really was. After all, God had set only one limitation—that they not eat from the Tree of the Knowledge of Good and Evil, because if they did so, they would surely die. But Eve goes a little further than what God had said. In her telling, God didn't simply say that they couldn't *eat* it. He said they couldn't *touch* it.

What difference does that make? Does God's command begin to seem slightly more unreasonable? What? You can't even *touch* the tree? Why not? How can touching it hurt anyone?

God didn't say anything about touching the tree. Eve also fails to name the tree the way God had. Does that make God look slightly more *arbitrary* in his command? Why did he pick out this one random tree in the middle of the garden and put restrictions on it? Even more subtly, Eve shaves a little bit off the consequences of transgressing God's command. He had said they would "certainly" die if they ate from the tree (2:17), but Eve leaves out the "certainly." How certain *is* the punishment, anyway?

So far, not much harm has been done. The serpent has asked a question, and Eve has answered it. She has been a little misleading and has slightly shaved the truth, but she hasn't outright lied, and the serpent hasn't called on her to do or believe anything different from what God said. But now, the serpent pushes forward more boldly. Sensing, ever so subtly, Eve's openness to think of things a little differently from what God has commanded, he goes in for the kill: "'You will not certainly die,' the serpent said to the woman" (3:4).

Now it's all or nothing for the serpent. Either Eve will be horrified at this direct contradiction of God's statement and repudiate him, or else she will keep the conversation going.

She doesn't interrupt. The serpent makes his sales pitch: "For God knows that when you eat from it your eyes will be opened, and you will be like God, knowing good and evil" (v. 5).

You will be like God! Who wouldn't want that? Now that the serpent has moved beyond subtle hints and is luring Eve into his trap directly, he offers the most dramatic benefit imaginable. His temptation is in full bloom. Eat the fruit and enjoy godlike powers. Furthermore, he points out that God knows this to be true. God is keeping that power from Eve! Why shouldn't she enjoy it? Eat! No modern advertiser could do a better job of turning something forbidden into something the consumer *deserves*.

Interestingly, the Bible does not record Eve's direct response to this. There seems to be an interval between verses 5 and 6. The story moves immediately from the serpent's words about becoming like God to one of the most fateful sentences in history: "When the woman saw that the fruit of the tree was good for food and pleasing to the eye, and also desirable for gaining wisdom, she took some and ate it" (v. 6).

How much time transpired between the serpent's evil enticement and that bite? Were they already standing near the tree, or did they have to walk some distance to get there? Did the serpent suggest they go look at it, or was that Eve's idea? Did the serpent continue to press his case as they walked, or did he stay quiet and let the seed of desire he had planted grow in Eve's mind?

It may seem strange that, given the consequences of her actions, she didn't offer more rebuttals or show more resistance to this invitation to contradict the only prohibition God had given in Paradise. But Eve was new to this. She was not used to being bombarded, as we are, by sales pitches from every direction to act in ways that are contrary to what God wants us to do. *Buy this*, we are told, even though it will mire you in a pit of debt from which it will take you years to crawl out. *Eat this*, even though it will harm your body. *Watch this*, even though it will warp your mind. Today, all of us are used to fending off—or falling prey to—countless temptations each day. Eve was a rookie to temptation.

Still, unlike us, she was unblemished by sin. She was pure, in ways that we are not. She needed to hold on to only one idea. God said this tree was forbidden. Instead, she gave in not only to the serpent's rationalizing but also to her own. Genesis 3:6 begins, "When the woman saw that the fruit of the tree was good for food and pleasing to the eye, and also desirable for gaining wisdom . . ." Does this thought process sound familiar? When I am trying to rationalize some bad behavior of my own that I am about to commit, I also like to come up with a list of why what I am about to do is really the right thing.

Eve set aside the only thing upon which she should have based her decision—God's command—and replaced it with her own preferences. The fruit was food, and food is good, right? The fruit is beautiful, and beauty is good, right? And also, as the serpent said, it would bring wisdom! Why should God have that treasure all to himself, especially when it was right there in front of her, ripe for the taking?

Come to think of it, why *did* God forbid Adam and Eve to eat the fruit from the Tree of the Knowledge of Good and Evil? It does seem understandable that she would want it. A good case could also be made for why God would want them to have this knowledge of good and evil that the fruit would provide. If it isn't useful, then why did he put it in the garden? Why take the risk that Adam and Eve would disobey?

No one knows why God put the tree there or why he prohibited the couple from eating from it. The point is that their obedience should not depend on their understanding of God's reasons for his command. Today, sin follows the same pattern. People put their own preferences ahead of God's commands. They second-guess his ways that seem odd or wrong in their limited human understanding.

Just because we don't understand God's reasons for something doesn't mean he doesn't *have* good reasons. Did God put the tree there simply as a test, to see whether Adam and Eve would really obey him? Or did he have a further purpose for that fruit? Some commentators have speculated that God's prohibition on eating from that tree was temporary and that he would lift it once he knew that Adam and Eve were ready to handle the knowledge its fruit would reveal. Wilbur Glenn Williams writes, "Had

Eve been patient and followed God's instruction, perhaps later God would have come to her and said, 'Eve, you can now go eat all of that fruit you want. You have shown that you understand obedience to Me to be more important than any other thing in life. You are now ready for it.'"[11]

Eve ate the fruit. The decision was hers alone. Although the serpent planted doubts about God in her mind and enticed her with what eating the fruit might do for her, she ultimately made her own choice. Scripture does not show the serpent dangling the fruit in front of her or pushing it on her.

Eve ate the fruit, and humanity would never be the same.

No one wants to sin alone. Bad behavior feels more acceptable, and the guilt more bearable, or easier to ignore, if other people are engaging in the same wrongdoing. Eve's first act after eating the fruit was to give some to her husband. The wording is significant: "She also gave some to her husband, who was with her, and he ate it" (v. 6). In case you forgot where Adam was during this whole episode, he wasn't off somewhere working the garden or hiking through the forest. He was right there with Eve! He could have said, "Stop! Don't do this. God has forbidden this, and I won't stand by silently while you make this tragic decision."

He said nothing. The serpent directed his persuasive tactics toward Eve, but Adam essentially assisted the serpent by standing by silently while Adam's soul mate, the woman who had been formed from his very own side, made the worst decision of her life.

Once she had eaten, it was much easier for Adam to follow along and eat the fruit also. She didn't have to persuade him. Neither did the serpent. The atmosphere was already full of rebellion against the Creator and his command, so Adam ate without comment. The fall of humanity was now fully initiated.

The Cover-Up

All of us know the impulse. We have done something wrong. We don't want to get caught. We also feel ashamed and want to hide that shame. This situation is familiar to us, but imagine the bewilderment of Adam and Eve, experiencing this guilt and shame for the first time. They were not sophisticated in how to handle it.

The statement in Genesis 3:7 that immediately follows Adam's sin is sad and ironic: "Then the eyes of both of them were opened, and they realized they were naked; so they sewed fig leaves together and made coverings for themselves." Their eyes were opened, just as the serpent had promised, but it was an opening that brought them only pain. Their nakedness, which they had experienced innocently their whole lives, now felt shameful, and they wanted to hide it.

They used fig leaves. That choice of leaf has become so famous that today the idea of putting a "fig leaf" over something means hiding the truth or concealing something with a lame excuse or cover story. In political scandals, it is often said that the cover-up is worse than the crime. Adam and Eve, like corrupt politicians, immediately worked to hide their offense. They took no time to reflect on the gravity of their guilt. They took no steps toward confessing to God or asking forgiveness from him. They immediately started covering themselves, both literally and figuratively. The literal cover-up required fig leaves, but they quickly realized their concerns about nakedness were nothing compared to what was coming next. God was entering the garden.

One enormous cost of their sin was that they lost their intimacy with God. Genesis 3:8 says, "Then the man and his wife heard the sound of the LORD God as he was walking in the garden in the cool of the day, and they hid from the LORD God among the trees of the garden." God knew what had happened already. Trying to hide from him—or hiding the truth from him—was as hopeless then as it is now. The description of God taking a walk "in the garden in the cool of the day" shows the familiarity that defined the relationship between the Creator and Adam and Eve. They were used to this physical manifestation of him right there with them. That is no doubt a big part of what made the place Paradise. How they must have longed for those times together in the past, but now, they felt ashamed. They hoped God wouldn't see them.

Their separation from God in that moment foreshadowed the separation of God from humanity that still exists today. People hide from him, they deny his existence, they pretend he is irrelevant, and they forget him. Adam and Eve were used to an intimacy with him that is hard for us to fathom. *God walked in the garden in the cool of the day.*

Given their close relationship to God, why didn't they throw themselves at his mercy and ask for forgiveness? They had done a terrible thing and needed rescue from the only one who could give it.

If Hiding Doesn't Work, Try Blaming Someone Else

Everyone else needs that spiritual rescue, too, but most of us have, at some point, or maybe even for our whole lives, resorted to trying to hide from God instead. For us, God is not walking in the garden. He may feel distant, and we have little trouble hiding, using all kinds of denial, rationalization, apathy, and other shields to block our view of him. But like a child who covers her eyes and believes that if she can't see her parent, the parent can't see her, we also falsely believe that if we block our awareness of God he inevitably forgets about us.

The hiding didn't last long for Adam and Eve. God knew where they were. He knew what they had done. Adam admits that he hid from God but says he was afraid because he was naked. But nakedness was not the problem.

His breaking of God's command was the problem, but Adam didn't want to talk about that. When God asked Adam whether he had eaten from the forbidden tree, Adam turned to another kind of familiar rationalization: "The woman you put here with me—she gave me some fruit from the tree, and I ate it" (Genesis 3:12). Shift the blame. If hiding doesn't work, if avoiding the real sin doesn't work, maybe blaming someone else will.

This woman you put here with me. Adam managed to blame not only Eve but also God in that statement. It was the woman's fault. It was also God's fault for putting the woman there in the first place. Sin disrupted the bond not only between the humans and God but also between Adam and Eve. He threw her under the bus.

God gave Eve a chance to come clean, but though she admitted her sin, she also couldn't resist mixing in some blame: "The woman said, 'The serpent deceived me, and I ate'" (v. 13).

Sin has consequences, and after Adam's and Eve's reluctant, blame-shifting confessions, the rest of Genesis 3 shows what those consequences would be. Some of them were immediate, and others were so long term that we are still suffering from them today.

No aspect of life escaped the repercussions of the fall. Adam and Eve were banished from their garden paradise. Work became hard and toilsome, as nature itself produced thorns and thistles. Childbirth became painful. Their relationships suffered. The serpent was punished. After Adam and Eve were ejected from the garden, cherubim were placed at its entrance to keep them and their descendants out.

Once Adam and Eve settled into their new life outside the garden, sin exploded. Genesis 4 tells of the horrific murder of their son Abel, committed by their son Cain, an act of evil that would have been unthinkable during their time in the garden. Generations of humanity continued to be born, as the genealogies in Genesis 5 highlight. By the time of Noah, many generations later, Genesis 6:5 declares that "the LORD saw how great the wickedness of the human race had become on the earth, and that every inclination of the thoughts of the human heart was only evil all the time."

The situation sounds about as dire as it could get, but even at the lowest points of the story, humanity was not without hope. Christian commentators have long found hope even in the immediate aftermath of Adam and Eve's sin in the garden. When he was punishing the serpent in Genesis 3:15, God said, "And I will put enmity between you and the woman, and between your offspring and hers; he will crush your head, and you will strike his heel." That offspring, many Christians believe, refers to Jesus Christ, who would crush Satan in Christ's crucifixion and resurrection. Already, as early as Genesis 3, the coming of Christ is prophesied, and there is hope for rescue.

God punished Adam and Eve, but he did not destroy them. They went on to live in a world that was fallen and sullied from sin, but they went on. He did not wipe them out and start from scratch. He gave them a second chance. Sin continued to thrive, but so did love.

What is the status of the fall today? Take a look around. It's an easy question to answer. Do you see the wars, the murders, the greed, the poverty, the injustice, the pettiness, selfishness, pride, mockery, pain, and death?

The story of the fall of Adam and Eve continues to reverberate. We can't forget the story or set it aside or move beyond it because we are still living it. We may make fun of it in our commercials or try to laugh it off in our jokes or try to tame it in our retellings and repaintings and reimaginings, but it continues to burn deep within us.

Although the depictions of Adam and Eve in current popular culture are often lighthearted or satirical, that is not always the case, and throughout history, the Adam and Eve story has often been portrayed with great reverence. One of the most powerful depictions of the story appears on one of Michelangelo's panels on the ceiling of the Vatican's Sistine Chapel. In his dramatic scene of humankind's fall in the garden of Eden, both the temptation and the expulsion from the garden are shown in the same panel. In the center is the serpent wrapped around the tree, reaching to hand the forbidden fruit to Eve to the left. Adam stands beside her. On the right side of the tree we see the aftermath of the tragedy, as an angel with a sword orders Adam and Eve away, their faces averted in shame, their bodies cowering.

It is a devastating scene, but an even more famous panel on that ceiling offers hope. In *The Creation of Adam*, the bearded God reaches out his hand toward Adam, who is also reaching toward God. Their hands almost touch. You have probably seen that image. You can probably picture it right now—God reaching out to humankind. It is a gesture of love from the almighty Creator to the first human being. God reaches out to give life to Adam. Those almost-touching hands have captured the imagination of the world.

Another influential treatment of the Adam and Eve story is John Milton's *Paradise Lost*, considered by many scholars to be "the greatest long poem in the English language."[12] Published in 1667, it is written in blank verse and is more than ten thousand lines long. *Paradise Lost* goes back even farther than the story of Adam and Eve, to Satan's rebellion against God, as Milton imagines it, which gets that fallen angel cast into hell. It also shows some of the aftermath of the fall, as Adam and Eve come to terms with one another and their altered status and hear prophecies of events to come, including Christ's sacrifice to bring humans salvation. Satan, who is a dominant and fascinating character in the poem, does not go quietly. He seeks his revenge by going after Adam and Eve. This poem includes details that go considerably beyond what the biblical story actually includes, and though the long poem is daunting for many readers today, it has nevertheless heavily influenced the popular perception of Satan, angels, Adam and Eve, and the fall of humanity.

Humanity Falls, but Hope Rises

For Christians, the fall of humankind, as tragic as it was, did not mean the end of hope. It meant that the intervention of Jesus Christ would be necessary. Adam and Eve show up a number of times in the New Testament. Paul in particular contrasts the consequences of the sin that came through Adam with the rescue that comes through Christ. In Romans 5:15 he writes, "For if the many died by the trespass of the one man, how much more did God's grace and the gift that came by the grace of the one man, Jesus Christ, overflow to the many!" In 1 Corinthians 15:22 he says, "For as in Adam all die, so in Christ all will be made alive."

Genesis 3 shows the loss of Eden and innocence and Paradise, but that is not the final word. Revelation 22 gives us the restoration of all those things in eternity:

Then the angel showed me the river of the water of life, as clear as crystal, flowing from the throne of God and of the Lamb down the middle of the great street of the city. On each side of the river stood the tree of life, bearing twelve crops of fruit, yielding its fruit every month. And the leaves of the tree are for the healing of the nations. No longer will there be any curse. (Vv. 1-3)

From Genesis to Revelation, the story of Adam and Eve is inescapable. For believers of the Bible, it is one of the most consequential stories ever told, a mixture of tragedy, hope, God's justice, and God's love. It's a story we cannot ignore.

Notes

1. "Adam and Eve Paintings," Fine Art America, accessed on December 31, 2018, https://fineartamerica.com/art/paintings/adam+and+eve?page=6.

2. Linda S. Schearing and Valarie H. Ziegler, *Enticed by Eden: How Western Culture Uses, Confuses (and Sometimes Abuses) Adam and Eve* (Waco, TX: Baylor University Press, 2013), 113.

3. "1974 Eve Cigarettes Ad—Bag and Belt Embroidery Kit," accessed on January 2, 2019, ebid, https://www.ebid.net/us/for-sale/1974-eve-cigarettes-ad-bag-and-belt-embroidery-kit-159239999.htm.

4. "Smirnoff the Apple Bite TV Commercial," YouTube video, 1:00, posted by "Aires De Bares," April 23, 2014, https://www.youtube.com/watch?v=ZIOqhBSE_zg.

5. "Adam and Eve," YouTube video, 0:34, posted by "CBS," February 1, 2011, https://www.youtube.com/watch?v=7DPFL0vr7iE.

6. Schearing and Ziegler, *Enticed by Eden*, 94.

7. Schearing and Ziegler, 96.

8. Schearing and Ziegler, 100.

9. Joseph Coleson, *Genesis 1–11*, New Beacon Bible Commentary (Kansas City: Beacon Hill Press of Kansas City, 2012), 102-3.

10. Coleson, 117.

11. Wilbur Glenn Williams, *Genesis: A Bible Commentary in the Wesleyan Tradition* (Indianapolis: Wesleyan Publishing House, 2000), 65.

12. William Kerrigan, John Rumrich, and Stephen M. Fallon, introduction to *Paradise Lost*, by John Milton (New York: Modern Library, 2007), ix.

Digging Deeper

1. This chapter shows a number of ways the Adam and Eve story has been used in advertising. Commercials and print ads twist the story, because in an ad, yielding to the temptation and buying the product being offered is seen as *success*, not moral failure. But in what ways do these ads also illustrate the spiritual lessons and truths about temptation and sin? How are the appeals the serpent makes to Eve similar to the ways advertisers appeal to readers and viewers?

2. God promises to create a "helper" for Adam. According to this chapter, what is the meaning of that term? Do you think that term is commonly misunderstood? If so, what are the implications and dangers of that misunderstanding?

3. This chapter points out that the biblical story spends little time describing the garden of Eden or showing what daily life was like for Adam and Eve before the temptation by the serpent. Why do you think Scripture spends so little time on that? What do you imagine life was like in Eden? Why was Paradise not enough for Adam and Eve?

Go to https://www.thefoundrypublishing.com/8OT/LeaderGuide for a free downloadable leader's guide that includes more questions for reflection as well as activities for use in a small group setting.

4

The Animals Enter Noah's Ark // Aurelio Luini // c. 1555

Noah and the Ark—
Not Just Cute Animals
on a Boat

⁹ *This is the account of Noah and his family.*

Noah was a righteous man, blameless among the people of his time, and he walked faithfully with God. ¹⁰ *Noah had three sons: Shem, Ham and Japheth.*

¹¹ *Now the earth was corrupt in God's sight and was full of violence.* ¹² *God saw how corrupt the earth had become, for all the people on earth had corrupted their ways.* ¹³ *So God said to Noah, "I am going to put an end to all people, for the earth is filled with violence because of them. I am surely going to destroy both them and the earth.* ¹⁴ *So make yourself an ark of cypress wood; make rooms in it and coat it with pitch inside and out.* ¹⁵ *This is how you are to build it: The ark is to be three hundred cubits long, fifty cubits wide and thirty cubits high.* ¹⁶ *Make a roof for it, leaving below the roof an opening one cubit high all around. Put a door in the side of the ark and make lower, middle and upper decks.* ¹⁷ *I am going to bring floodwaters on the earth to destroy all life under the heavens, every creature that has the breath of life in it. Everything on earth will perish.* ¹⁸ *But I will establish my covenant with you, and you will enter the ark—you and your sons and your wife and your sons' wives with you.* ¹⁹ *You are to bring into the ark two of all living creatures, male and female, to keep them alive with you.* ²⁰ *Two of every kind of bird, of every kind of animal and of every kind of creature that moves along the ground will come to you to be kept alive.* ²¹ *You are to take every kind of food that is to be eaten and store it away as food for you and for them."*

²² *Noah did everything just as God commanded him.*

—*Genesis 6:9-22*

LIKE MANY PEOPLE, when I hear the phrase "Noah and the ark," I picture a kids' cartoon version of the story, with a grandfatherly, white-bearded Noah holding a staff as he leads the smiling pairs of giraffes, elephants, kangaroos, zebras, alligators, birds, and other animals into a spacious wooden ark. A flood may be coming, but they'll all be safe and cozy inside this big boat as they wait for the rain to stop, the water to recede, and the rainbow to appear.

A vast array of products with that same happy vision of the story, mostly targeted toward children, have been created to celebrate Noah and his animals. How vast? One website, Etsy, offers more than ten thousand Noah-related products. Think of that for a moment. If you sat me down and told me to think of even one thousand *possible* products that could fit this category, I doubt if I could do it, and yet this online store sells ten times that.

What do they sell? Noah's ark baptism candles, with a colorful ark, a rainbow, and animals carved into each candle; Noah's ark clip art; and a T-shirt that says, "Need an ark? I Noah guy." Other items with the Noah's ark theme include key chains, cake toppers, coloring books, pendants, a wooden ark model, rainbow-decorated water bottles (filled with rainwater), clothes-closet dividers, piggy banks, burp cloths, ceramic figurines, Christmas tree ornaments, tablecloths, paintings, gift tags, quilts, baby blankets, magnets, and coffee mugs. The list could go on for many pages.

Etsy is far from the only company to see the marketing potential of Noah and his boatful of animals. If you have $110 to spare, you can buy a colorful Noah's Ark Wooden Play Set from the Met Store. Fisher-Price sells a much cheaper Little People Noah's Ark, with plastic animals, a plastic Noah, and a plastic ark for toddlers. The deck of the ark comes off so the children can play with the animals inside it. The Holy Land Experience offers a cute and cuddly cloth version of the ark, with stuffed animals that can peek out from the windows. The Catholic Company sells a Noah's Ark Playset and an accompanying book that tells the story.

If our culture is willing to put the Noah's ark story on baby bibs and party favors, what does that say about how we view the story? It's cute. It's precious. It's a floating zoo, and once the cruise is over, a rainbow pops up! What could be more adorable?

The story in Genesis, however, is not cute or adorable. Although God's love and redemption are ultimately at its core, it is also one of the most disturbing and frightening stories in the Bible. Consider Genesis 6:5-7:

> The Lord saw how great the wickedness of the human race had become on the earth, and that every inclination of the thoughts of the human heart was only evil all the time. The Lord regretted that he had made human beings on the earth, and his heart was deeply troubled. So the Lord said, "I will wipe from the face of the earth the human race I have created—and with them the animals, the birds and the creatures that move along the ground—for I regret that I have made them."

The story of Noah is set in a world of pervasive evil. Not all of that evil is detailed. The Genesis account does not show most of it, so we are left to imagine what a depraved place the world must have become. God is ready to obliterate his creation that had been so beautiful. In many ways this is one of the lowest points in the entire story of the Bible. Even after the tragic fall of Adam and Eve, God did not speak of ending his creation. Now he is ready to do so.

God does not take that shocking and drastic step—Noah finds favor in his eyes—but the response he does choose is still hard to fathom. The wickedness that had overtaken the world had to be swept aside, the earth washed clean with the deluge that would rid God's creation of the blot of evil. The human race, along with the animals and the rest of creation, would be given a new start. The long-term plan was the redemption of all creation, but the flood was no children's story of smiling animals marching two by two into Grandfather Noah's big boat for an exciting ride. Instead, it was a story of suffering and death: bodies floating on the water, people and animals swept away and drowned, plants and trees uprooted, houses crushed, and villages abolished.

That harsh version of Noah's story hasn't caught on too much in the popular imagination. It's easy to see why. Who wants to buy burp cloths decorated with bodies floating through a flooded village? Who wants drowned animals on their baby blankets, or tablecloths decorated with screaming men and women pounding on the ark as the waters rise?

If you're teaching a Sunday school class for children or writing a children's Bible story book or designing a product for sale for kids and their parents on a website, you're much more likely to lean toward the details of this story that kids will love: animals, a big boat, an exciting flood, a dove with an olive branch, and a rainbow.

Retelling Noah's Story to Children

Hundreds of children's books retell the story of Noah and the ark. The younger the target audience, the more the authors and illustrators downplay the disturbing parts of the story. A board book called *The Story of Noah* avoids any mention of the wickedness of the people that leads to the flood. It simply begins, "A long time ago God said to Noah, 'You must build a boat.'"[1] Noah does so, even though his friends laugh at him for constructing a boat in the desert. Noah fills his boat with adorable, smiling creatures. The storm comes, the boat floats, but no mention is made of other people. The water recedes, the land is clean and dry, and the book ends with Noah seeing the first rainbow.

Some versions of the story targeted toward older children handle the unpleasant part of the story with a little more complexity. Jerry Pinkney's *Noah's Ark*, a Caldecott Honor Book, features beautiful, intricate illustrations: the frame of the ark under construction, richly detailed animals, storm waters vividly rising up to the ark, and so on. The text, like the drawings, is not all about beauty. The story begins, "God was not pleased with the people of the earth. They did not care for one another. They did not care for the land that God had made. And they did not care for God."[2] That is a pretty good summary of the Genesis account's explanation for the flood. This version follows the biblical account, but the suffering of those left behind is only hinted at: "The water rose over cities and towns. Whales swam down ruined streets. Schools of fish darted through empty windows."[3] Ruined streets and empty windows, but what about people? They're dead but not mentioned. The story's attention quickly turns to Noah and the animals.

I did find one children's book that offered hints of the human tragedy that is part of the Noah story. *Noah's Ark*, written by Heinz Janisch, illustrated by Lisbeth Zwerger, and translated by Rosemary Lanning, says that "God saw that His people had grown wicked. They thought only of war and destruction."[4] This is depicted with a drawing of a hilly but barren landscape strewn with oversized bones, weapons of war, and buildings topped with huge plumes of smoke. The people in this story's illustrations wear modern clothing. Once the flood hits, one small image shows people cowering on top of the roof of a home in which the floodwater now has risen halfway up the windows. A larger image on the facing page shows people with umbrellas straining against the wind, as the ark floats in the distant background and a white unicorn gallops across the page.[5]

Children's Story? Horror Story? Redemption Story?

At its core, what *is* Noah's story? An adventure tale? A children's story? A disaster narrative? A horror story? Why is it in the Bible, and what should we do with it?

One important point to keep in mind is that the Noah story is not told in isolation. It is part of the Genesis 1–11 narrative, which functions as what Joseph Coleson and other biblical commentators have called a kind of "prologue" to the rest of Scripture. Coleson writes that this section of Genesis "gives a theological perspective on the beginnings of human alienation from God, from each other, from ourselves individually and internally, and from the rest of creation. It assures us God did not give up on humans then, nor will God do so now."[6] The Noah story is the culmination of a string of human failures and disobedience. The wickedness started with the fall of Adam and Eve, ratcheted up with Cain's murder of Abel, and then steadily increased throughout the generations leading up to the days of Noah.

Genesis is not alone in telling the story of an ancient flood. Dozens of flood narratives survive from many cultures around the world, such as the one told in the *Epic of Gilgamesh*. Many of these stories have similarities to the Genesis account, but many differ in significant ways. The repetition across cultures shows the importance of this account to people throughout history. Like the rest of the stories in the opening chapters of Genesis, the Noah story not only contains content that other cultures would recognize but is also told in a manner that was more familiar to people of the ancient Near East than it is to us today. Commentator Brad E. Kelle explains that the stories throughout Genesis 1–11 "describe a type of primeval history—a sort of world before time—marked by idyllic gardens, talking animals, great floods, and divine beings who intermarry with humans. These descriptions are not usually the ways that we talk about the nature of the world and the origins of life today (and they have little in common with what modern scientific study says, as well)."[7] The stories throughout these opening chapters of Genesis have been gathered together "in a way that invites us to see the different perspectives and portrayals as part of a larger story that begins with God's intentions, humanity's failures, and God's responses, and then carries on through the calling, creation, and formation of a people in the remainder" of the first five books of the Bible.[8]

Humans might have hoped that the offspring of Adam and Eve, having seen the devastating consequences of sin their parents faced, would have considered that loss of Eden as they decided how to build the world in which they had been given a second chance. The world was fallen, and sin was not going away, but humans still had choices about how they treated one another and how they cared for the still magnificent creation God had given them. Not even one generation chose wisely. By the time of Noah, evil had accelerated to such a point that not only had human beings reached a level of corruption that was beyond what God could tolerate, but those humans had wrecked the rest of his creation also.

God could have chosen many methods to eliminate the evil that now pervaded the world—fire, earthquake, plague. Water was his choice. It would destroy but also cleanse. The dirt, the sin, would be washed away. However, God would not annihilate all of creation and then later start from scratch. As Genesis 6:8 says, "But Noah found favor in the eyes of the LORD." God's grief over sin is mixed inextricably with his intention to renew and redeem. In the middle of dry land, he orders the construction of an ark.

The Ark: Graceful Ship or Floating Box?

Genesis gives the dimensions of this extraordinary floating box—about 450 feet long, 75 feet wide, and 45 feet high[9]—but it is not described in detail. People have interpreted it in many different ways in paintings, models, and toys. One group has even re-created a life-size version of the ark based on biblical specifications. The Ark Encounter in Kentucky is a full-size ark that is more than one and a half football fields long and big enough to fit a three-story museum inside, with live animals, dozens of exhibits, re-created living quarters for Noah's family, and other highlights. It is advertised as "the largest timber frame structure in the world, built from standing dead timber, in part by skilled Amish craftsmen."[10]

The ark in Kentucky is beautiful and intricately shaped and designed, but others who have re-created the ark have interpreted it as a more rough-hewn structure, particularly considering the primitive era in which it was built. In the 2014 film *Noah*, for example, the ark is boxy, rough-timbered, and slathered in pitch. It looks homemade, and its chances of surviving the deluge that was about to hit it seem questionable. Whatever the ark may have looked like, it did not need any mechanisms for steering or navigating, and none are described for Noah to build. He would not steer the ark. He simply had to take care of his family and the animals while the flood took it in whatever direction God might lead.

The ark, which has captivated the imaginations of everyone from children in Sunday school to Hollywood filmmakers, is also a key symbol of faith. It represents the total dependence on God that Noah, his family, and even the animals had to accept. The story is one of the most famous ones in the Bible, but like so many others in Scripture, it is sparsely told. Noah's emotional reactions to God's extraordinary commands are not recorded.

Think of it. God shows up and tells Noah of his plans for destruction, orders the construction of a preposterously large boat, tells about the animals that will come in pairs to join Noah and his family on the ark, and gives instructions for storing enough food on the ark for the humans and the animals. Noah might have responded in many ways: fear, incredulity, anger, reluctance, hostility. He could have bargained, he could have procrastinated, and he could have told God to find someone else. Instead, the only response that Genesis records is this: "Noah did everything just as God commanded him" (6:22).

In the next chapter, once the ark is built—a process that must have been horrendously difficult but that is not detailed in Scripture—God gives further instructions about loading the family and animals onto the ark. This is also a task of obviously intense complexity, but once again, the only record of Noah's response is, "And Noah did all that the LORD commanded him" (7:5). That rock-solid faith and dependence on God would be needed to get Noah and his family through the upcoming days, weeks, and months of this ordeal. Noah was not told how long the flood would last, how long it would take for the waters to recede, or what would happen after that. He simply rode this homemade vessel and trusted God to keep it afloat and guide it to where it needed to be. He could not rescue those who perished outside the ark. He followed the Lord's instructions, but the outcome was out of his hands. He was, as Genesis 6:9 records, "a righteous man, blameless among the people of his time, and he walked faithfully with God." He obeyed God, he trusted him, and he waited for the outcome.

The Genesis account of the flood emphasizes the destruction but does not detail it. "Everything on dry land that had the breath of life in its nostrils died," Genesis 7:22 matter-of-factly records. Not only are the specifics of the suffering outside the ark not provided, but daily life inside the ark is not recorded either. We know only that the trip was long. Vast amounts of water gushed from "the springs of the great deep" (v. 11), and torrents of rain poured from the "floodgates of the heavens" (v. 11) nonstop for forty days and nights. That water would kill everything, and Noah and his family would have to start from nothing once the water receded, but that receding did not come quickly.

Even after forty days of constant rain and the deluge of waters from the deep, more than five more months passed before the waters *began* to recede. Every part of the Noah story is a combination of suffering and hope. God was destroying, but he had renewal in motion as well. The ark did not sink. The people and animals did not die. Eventually the waters went down enough for the ark to rest on the mountains of Ararat. That didn't mean Noah and the animals could jump out and start their new lives. The world was still a waterlogged, ruined mess. As Coleson describes it, "With the flood, God had de-created the earth, reversing God's good creation all the way back to its earliest state of all-encompassing water and darkness. . . . Now, with the receding of the waters, the narrator reports a second reversal. Out of the *de*-creation God *re*-created."[11]

This process took time, not just to rebuild later on, but even simply to leave the ark. The land dried for months. As the days wore on, Noah eventually sent out a dove to see if the land was dry enough to sustain life. At first the dove returned, but eventually one day it came back carrying a fresh olive branch in its beak. New life! When he sent it out after that, it did not return. That was a happy sign. The animal had left the ark for good to start a new life, and it was time for the humans and other animals to do so too.

A Covenant, a Rainbow—but Disturbing Signs Too

The next part of the story includes some of the most positive elements, but even then, ominous signs and events are built into it. Noah gets off to a good start when he and his family and the animals leave the ark. He builds an altar and makes a sacrifice to the Lord. God is attentive. He doesn't simply let the humans and animals go off to fend for themselves the best way they can. He performs what Brad Kelle calls "a single, destiny-altering divine act that puts a new reality into place for God, humanity, and all creation: covenant."[12] God's covenant offers a fresh start for this new, post-flood world, and it sets in place his plan for the redemption of his creation.

Making a covenant is something God does only a few times in Scripture. This covenant, which he declares in Genesis 9:7-11, encompasses not only one person, not only one family, not only one tribe or nation, but all humanity from that time forward. It also is not only for humans. Those animals who rode in the ark? They're included too. The covenant is with his whole creation. God promises not to destroy the earth by flood ever again. Then he does something that has helped make this story such a Sunday school and children's book favorite: he sets a rainbow in the sky. But that rainbow isn't some sentimental ending to a sweet kids' story. Or at least that's not *all* it is. It is a sign from God that his heart is set—for the long term, for redemption, for restoration, for new life, and for new possibilities. That's the hope that springs from the story.

Echoing language from the creation story at the beginning of Genesis, God blesses Noah and his sons and tells them, "Be fruitful and increase in number and fill the earth" (9:1). He gives them animals and plants for food. God's creation is once again set for flourishing. In Kelle's words, "Genesis 9 envisions a return to the original conditions of blessing, fertility, and flourishing described in Genesis 1—a universal redemptive promise for all of creation."[13] All in all, it sounds like a happy ending, except . . .

I hate to interrupt this rainbow moment, but disturbing signs appear in the story even before the ground has dried from the receding water. Even at one of the high points of the story, when God is about to bless Noah and his sons and is promising never again to "curse the ground because of humans," he says that he is making that promise "even though every inclination of the human heart is evil from childhood" (8:21). Hmm. That pessimistic declaration does not bode well, and the humans who have survived the flood—these are the relatively good ones, remember—soon prove God right.

Only a few short verses after God speaks of the covenant between himself and all life on earth, Noah—our hero, Noah—ends up drunk and naked in his tent, and his youngest son does something disgraceful against him. Has it really all turned bad again so quickly? As a reader, I long to see at least a chapter or two of happiness and harmony in this newly launched world. God has offered a fresh start, but human beings are still sinful, and they still need saving.

How will God accomplish that? Christians believe it takes the entire rest of the Bible to answer that question, with highlights such as the covenant with Abraham and Sarah and their descendants, the coming of Jesus Christ with his death and resurrection, the establishment of the church at the coming of the Holy Spirit, and the end-time events that will establish ultimate restoration in eternity. It will take a long time for God to set things right. The journey to redemption will be marred by endless human failure and evil in the midst of stunning outpourings of God's love. Noah's story, with its highs and lows, is a foreshadowing of the centuries of tumultuous events that will follow it.

Noah Goes to the Movies: Filling in the Gaps

The Genesis account of Noah and the ark is one of the most well-known stories in the world, but that biblical account of it leaves gaps that modern filmmakers and other storytellers find irresistible to fill in. How did Noah manage to get all those animals into the ark? What did he *think* about the commands God gave him? What did he *say*? (None of Noah's words are recorded in Genesis until the end, when he curses his son.) Exactly what kind of evil was happening at the time of the flood? What did the people around Noah think about this ark that was being built?

One of the most impressive movie versions of the story is the 2014 film *Noah*, starring Russell Crowe.[14] It doesn't please everyone in some of the ways it fills in the gaps with story elements from extrabiblical sources, but it provides a thought-provoking portrayal of the evil that pervaded the world in the days before the flood. The film makes clear that the Noah story should not be viewed in isolation from what precedes it in Genesis. The movie opens with scenes and text from earlier parts of Genesis, including Adam and Eve and their fall to temptation, Cain's killing of his brother Abel, the spread of civilization, and the increasing corruption that festered in the following generations.

Many versions of the Noah story downplay the violence of Noah's day, but this film shows it in abundance. As a child, Noah watches evil men kill his father. Much later, when Noah and his wife and sons travel on foot to find his grandfather Methuselah, they cross a barren, blasted landscape and come across the bodies of villagers whose town has been looted. Raiders chase them past piles of skulls and skeletons on stakes. Later scenes, closer to the time of the flood, show the appalling camps of the corrupt king Tubal-Cain, where screaming women are bought and sold for food and where people live in squalor, rage, and fear.

The wickedness is so pervasive that Noah becomes convinced that God intends to destroy all of humanity, including himself and his family, and save only the animals. "The time for mercy is past," he tells his wife. "Now our punishment begins." Later, on the ark, when Noah tells his family the story of how God created the world and how Adam and Eve and later generations ruined it, he says, "We broke the world. We did this. Man did this. Everything that was beautiful, everything that was good, we shattered. Now, it begins again." He adds, "Paradise returns, but this time, there will be no men. Mankind must end."[15] Genesis makes clear that God intends to form a covenant with Noah that will offer hope to humanity and the rest of creation, but in the film, Noah is so aware of the sin of humans that he has a hard time believing that God will allow them to continue. His views on that are eventually challenged, but the film's interpretation of Noah's initial cynicism about the future of humanity emphasizes that he knows, as the Genesis account also shows, that even he and his family are not immune from the corruption that has ruined the world. God will start fresh with his family, but the postflood era will not be a return to the paradise of Eden.

The flood story is, among other things, one of the most dramatic action-adventure episodes in all the Bible, and *Noah* emphasizes those elements. In some retellings of the story, Noah's neighbors are portrayed as responding with mockery and sarcasm to his building of the ark, but in this film, the soldiers and other citizens sense the catastrophe that is coming and want access to Noah's vessel. For one thing, they see the amazing arrival of various types of animals. While the ark is still under construction, massive flocks of birds fly into the ark and take their places. Noah and his family sedate them and the other animals that arrive with a smoke that puts them to sleep. Snakes, lizards, and insects creep in. Later, bigger animals such as elephants and bears arrive and are sedated.

The citizens around Noah, living in a land that is barren and villages that are unlivable, don't want to get left behind. They are willing to storm the ark to get in, but when the time comes, they are prevented and are washed away. As water bursts up from the ground, drowning soldiers, the ark itself is almost submerged, but the crude vessel survives, while those within hear the screams of those dying outside.

A Modern, Reluctant Noah Who Can't Escape God's Call

One of the most popular film adaptations of the Noah story takes a very different approach. *Evan Almighty*, a 2007 comedy starring Steve Carell as the Noah character, is a modern version of the story in which Evan

Baxter is a newly elected congressman who won his seat with "Change the World" as his slogan. God pursues the reluctant Evan to build the ark, and the congressman cannot escape his call. He starts seeing "6:14" everywhere. His alarm clock is set for 7:00 a.m. but goes off at 6:14 a.m. instead. He sees the number on a protest poster, a license plate, the weight of a newborn baby, and elsewhere. He eventually finds that the numbers refer to Genesis 6:14, in which God orders Noah to build the ark; however, he tries to escape the implications of what the signs may mean.

Lumber and other building supplies are delivered to his house even though he hasn't ordered them. Animals, in pairs, follow him to Capitol Hill. Birds fly into his office. He confronts animals everywhere. Snakes slither on him, and he finds sheep in the back seat of his car. His face spontaneously begins to grow a beard that makes him look like the Noah figure from the children's stories, and he can't shave it off. His life is greatly inconvenienced, his family is confused, and his work as a new congressman is put in jeopardy, since all of it is so embarrassing and hard to explain to anyone. God, in the form of Morgan Freeman (who else?), tells him, "Whatever I do, I do because I love you."[16]

As a comedy, *Evan Almighty* avoids most of the violent and painful aspects of the Genesis version of Noah. Without giving too many spoilers, it's safe to say that people aren't left dead outside the ark. In its own way, this version illustrates a lesson of faith, as Evan comes to terms with the idea that he really can trust God. It also teaches other lessons. Evan's sons learn to appreciate him much more as the eccentric Noah figure who spends quality time with them building the ark than they did when he was a busy congressman who ignored them. It's a feel-good movie, but just as the 6:14 references finally push Evan to read the biblical account, this movie may do the same for some viewers.

The Noah story continues to be influential for people of various ages and cultures not just because it's a cute children's tale with animals, a boat, and a rainbow but also because it deals with the biggest issues of life—humanity's propensity to sin, our deep need for redemption, and God's determination to confront evil and offer a better way. The story deals in extremes—enormous cataclysm and intimate covenant between God and his creation. It does not shy away from horror and destruction, but ultimately, it signals hope.

Notes

1. Patricia A. Pingry, *The Story of Noah*, illus. Stacy Venturi-Pickett (Nashville: Ideals Publications, 1977), n.p.

2. Jerry Pinkney, *Noah's Ark* (New York: SeaStar Books, 2002), n.p.

3. Pinkney, n.p.

4. Heinz Janisch, *Noah's Ark*, illus. Lisbeth Zwerger, trans. Rosemary Lanning (New York: North-South Books, 1997), n.p.

5. Janisch, n.p.

6. Joseph Coleson, *Genesis 1–11*, New Beacon Bible Commentary (Kansas City: Beacon Hill Press of Kanas City, 2012), 24.

7. Brad E. Kelle, *Telling the Old Testament Story: God's Mission and God's People* (Nashville: Abingdon Press, 2017), 31.

8. Kelle, 32.

9. Coleson, *Genesis 1–11*, 211.

10. "A Massive Structure," Arkencounter.com, accessed on April 22, 2021, https://ark encounter.com/about/.

11. Coleson, *Genesis 1–11*, 231.

12. Kelle, *Telling the Old Testament Story*, 51.

13. Kelle, 52.

14. *Noah*, directed by Darren Aronofsky (Hollywood, CA: Paramount Pictures, 2014), Amazon Prime Video.

15. *Noah*, directed by Aronofsky.

16. *Evan Almighty*, directed by Tom Shadyac (Universal City, CA: Universal Pictures, 2007), Amazon Prime Video.

Digging Deeper

1. This chapter considers the ways some children's books retell the story of Noah and the ark. What do you think about the ways that these and other children's versions handle the disturbing parts of the story, such as the evil that leads to the flood or the deaths caused by the flood? How should books for children handle those issues? What spiritual themes and lessons from the Noah story would be helpful to children?

2. God asks Noah to do outlandish things: build a huge boat, gather animals, and prepare for a flood of incredible proportions. As this chapter says, "Noah might have responded in many ways: fear, incredulity, anger, reluctance, hostility. He could have bargained, . . . procrastinated, and . . . told God to find someone else. Instead, the only response that Genesis records is this: 'Noah did everything just as God commanded him' (6:22)." What does this tell us about Noah and why God may have chosen him? Could he have had some of those negative reactions, but Scripture did not record them? How would you have responded if you were in Noah's place?

3. This chapter asks, "At its core, what *is* Noah's story? An adventure tale? A children's story? A disaster narrative? A horror story? Why is it in the Bible, and what should we do with it?" What do you believe is the essence of the Noah story? Do you think it is widely misunderstood?

Go to https://www.thefoundrypublishing.com/8OT/LeaderGuide for a free downloadable leader's guide that includes more questions for reflection as well as activities for use in a small group setting.

5

Naomi Entreating Ruth and Orpah to Return to the Land of Moab // William
Blake // 1795

Ruth—Where You Go
I Will Go

¹ *In the days when the judges ruled, there was a famine in the land. So a man from Bethlehem in Judah, together with his wife and two sons, went to live for a while in the country of Moab.* ² *The man's name was Elimelek, his wife's name was Naomi, and the names of his two sons were Mahlon and Kilion. They were Ephrathites from Bethlehem, Judah. And they went to Moab and lived there.*

³ *Now Elimelek, Naomi's husband, died, and she was left with her two sons.* ⁴ *They married Moabite women, one named Orpah and the other Ruth. After they had lived there about ten years,* ⁵ *both Mahlon and Kilion also died, and Naomi was left without her two sons and her husband.*

⁶ *When Naomi heard in Moab that the* Lord *had come to the aid of his people by providing food for them, she and her daughters-in-law prepared to return home from there.* ⁷ *With her two daughters-in-law she left the place where she had been living and set out on the road that would take them back to the land of Judah.*

⁸ *Then Naomi said to her two daughters-in-law, "Go back, each of you, to your mother's home. May the* Lord *show you kindness, as you have shown kindness to your dead husbands and to me.* ⁹ *May the* Lord *grant that each of you will find rest in the home of another husband."*

Then she kissed them goodbye and they wept aloud ¹⁰ *and said to her, "We will go back with you to your people."*

¹¹ *But Naomi said, "Return home, my daughters. Why would you come with me? Am I going to have any more sons, who could become your husbands?* ¹² *Return home, my daughters; I am too old to have another husband. Even if I thought there was still hope for me—even if I had a husband tonight and then gave birth to sons—* ¹³ *would you wait until they grew up? Would you remain unmarried for them? No, my daughters. It is more bitter for me than for you, because the* Lord's *hand has turned against me!"*

¹⁴ *At this they wept aloud again. Then Orpah kissed her mother-in-law goodbye, but Ruth clung to her.*

¹⁵ *"Look," said Naomi, "your sister-in-law is going back to her people and her gods. Go back with her."*

¹⁶ *But Ruth replied, "Don't urge me to leave you or to turn back from you. Where you go I will go, and where you stay I will stay. Your people will be my people and your God my God.* ¹⁷ *Where you die I will die, and there I will be buried. May the* Lord *deal with me, be it ever so severely, if even death separates you and me."* ¹⁸ *When Naomi realized that Ruth was determined to go with her, she stopped urging her.*

—*Ruth 1:1-18*

"YOU HAVE TO INCLUDE THE BOOK OF RUTH." That's what people kept telling me as I talked to friends and colleagues about what Old Testament passages and stories I planned to focus on in this book. I was reluctant at first, since the Old Testament is too big to write about every important passage in it. I started with passages and figures I thought had the greatest impact on literature, popular culture, art, advertising, law, and other aspects of life. I wrote chapters on biblical giants—Moses, Abraham, David. These were people who changed the history of the world. They were larger-than-life figures who heard directly from God. Abraham rose from obscurity to a place of reverence that he holds even today among Jews, Christians, and Muslims. Moses defied Pharaoh, parted a sea, and led his people to the promised land. David slew Goliath and triumphed as king of Israel.

The story of Ruth, by comparison, comes across as smaller and more personal. Two women, Ruth and Naomi, down on their luck, feeling abandoned and without clear direction, search for a way out of their money problems. Their husbands have died. They have to make a long journey to a place where they don't fit in. The future looks bleak.

That story isn't exactly Noah building an ark or Moses defying Pharaoh or David killing a giant. However, although most people will never be called on to build a large boat or defeat a world leader or slay a man by propelling a stone at his head, many people *do* face some version of the problems Naomi and Ruth endure. Millions of people have money problems. Millions lose loved ones or find their formerly hopeful futures blotted out or feel trampled by a society that doesn't think they have much value.

When I mentioned to one of my colleagues that the book of Ruth had not, like other biblical stories, inspired prominent films like *The Ten Commandments* or famous sculptures like Michelangelo's *David*, and that people don't buy themed wallpaper and toys for Ruth as they do for Noah's ark, he said my perspective was too narrowly American. He pointed me to the work of Philip Jenkins, who has studied Christianity in the Global South—that is, Latin America, Africa, and Asia. While the book of Ruth may be respected in the United States and other prosperous cultures, it is *beloved* in the Global South. For many of us, details of the book of Ruth, such as gleaning, the marriage rituals, the threats of poverty, and the close ties to the land, make a compelling story, but they are *someone else's* story.

However, for Christians in some economically poor areas of the Global South, those issues are everyday realities. Jenkins writes that in those regions, the book of Ruth "becomes a model, even a manual, for a situation that could arise all too easily."[1] He quotes a writer named Musimbi Kanyoro, who explains, "The book of Ruth is loved because it has something for everyone in Africa. Africans read this book in a context in which famine, . . . , levirate marriages and polygamy are not ancient biblical practices but normal realities of today."[2]

In a poor migrant refugee camp in Indonesia in the mid-1990s, the book of Ruth was chosen for study at the rate of a chapter a week. A missionary reported that the widows in this community formed their own widows group and felt a strong connection to the women in the story. "The biblical novelette of failure in economic migration brought out stories of the dead-end life that the women were leading in the Patisomba transit station. The strategy which the resilient Naomi and Ruth drew up and carried out successfully fired their imaginations. On the final Sunday, they presented their findings to the whole congregation in a series of dramatic declamations."[3] The young people in this refugee community also studied Ruth in their own group and presented the story in dramatized form.

Seeing the way readers in refugee camps and in famine-stricken lands relate to this story brought me a fresh perspective on how much is at stake for Naomi and Ruth. It's easy for me to tame this story, since it is so familiar and I know that everything's going to turn out all right. But these women do not know that. They are caught in a desperate financial and social trap, in a world that was tough on women. No husbands, no financial support, no clear future.

Before you think of the story any further, imagine your own finances stripped away, your family and other support network obliterated, your opportunities for independence curtailed by societal structures that exclude you. No wonder Naomi calls herself "Mara," which means "Bitter" (Ruth 1:20). No wonder she feels abandoned by God. No wonder she expects—and even urges—the daughters-in-law to leave her too.

The Story of Women at Life's Lowest Moments

The book of Ruth is a story about women. Although the Old Testament includes the stories of many fascinating women—Eve, Sarah, Esther, Deborah, Rahab, Hannah, and others—few other books put women at the center of the story the way the book of Ruth does. Unlike figures such as

Noah, Abraham, or Moses, the stories of Ruth and Naomi are not set in motion by hearing God's voice and then responding to his direction. Instead, desperation is their guide at first. God seems far away, even hostile, in Naomi's view. They start their journey on their own and discover God's presence only when they reach their lowest point.

Naomi's difficulties begin long before the deaths of her husbands and sons. At the beginning of the book, her family is forced to leave their hometown of Bethlehem and go to a place where they will be outsiders and strangers—Moab.

In the understated tone so common in the Old Testament, the first verse reveals that in the time when the judges ruled, "there was a famine in the land. So a man from Bethlehem in Judah, together with his wife and two sons, went to live for a while in the country of Moab" (Ruth 1:1). That may not sound like such a disaster in our day, when people move from place to place rather routinely, but here the famine must have been severe indeed to cause them to flee the place where generations of their family had lived. To give up land, family, their place of worship—everything. How would they be received in this new place? How would they survive? They plan for it to be temporary, but it doesn't turn out that way for some of them.

All of that happens in just the first verse. In the second verse, we learn that Naomi's husband's name is Elimelek, and that they have two sons, Mahlon and Kilion. In the third verse, Elimelek dies. In the fourth verse, the sons marry Moabite women, Orpah and Ruth, and live with them for ten years. In the fifth verse, both men die, leaving Naomi without husband or sons, and her daughters-in-law without husbands or children. In five short verses, all is lost, and the future looks bleak. As Phyllis Trible says of Naomi, "From wife to widow, from mother to no-mother, this female is stripped of all identity. The security of husband and children, which a male-dominated culture affords its women, is hers no longer. The definition of worth, by which it values the female, applies to her no more. The blessings of old age, which it gives through progeny, are there no longer."[4]

The gloom lifts a bit in the sixth verse, but the news the women receive isn't enough to fill Naomi with hope. She finds out that "the LORD had come to the aid of his people by providing food for them," so she and Ruth and Orpah decide to go back to the land Naomi had come from. They actually set off toward Judah, but for reasons the text does not state, Naomi changes her mind about bringing these women with her. While on the road, she reluctantly turns to them and urges them to go back to Moab.

If the three women were going to go their separate ways, it would have made more sense to do it *before* they started their journey. I can't help but wonder why Naomi let Ruth and Orpah go part of the way before she confronted them. One reason might be Naomi's understandable reluctance to travel alone on such a dangerous journey. Everything about her interaction with these two women indicates her deep love for them and their love for her. After all that Naomi had already lost, it must have been hard to contemplate losing these close family members too. She does not want to leave them, and they don't want to leave her. I imagine all three women started on this journey hoping, in spite of all they knew about how their world worked, that they could somehow stick together and make a good life in Naomi's hometown of Bethlehem.

Naomi, somewhere on that road, finally faces reality. It doesn't make sense for these daughters-in-law to come with her instead of finding new husbands in their own homeland. Several verses later, Naomi will name herself "Bitter" (see v. 20), and that has always made me picture her as a grouchy and morose woman. But when I look carefully at that scene on the road, when she urges Ruth and Orpah to leave her and go back to Moab, I see love. Naomi has nothing personally to gain by turning the daughters away. If she were thinking only about herself, she could have waited until they arrived safely in Bethlehem before she contemplated their futures. She realizes it isn't fair to put them through this. There is no future for them where she is going.

"Go back, each of you," she urges, "to your mother's home. May the LORD show you kindness, as you have shown kindness to your dead husbands and to me. May the LORD grant that each of you will find rest in the home of another husband" (vv. 8-9). When she kisses them goodbye, they weep loudly and insist that they will continue on with her. She has to plead with them even more strenuously to get them to see that their only hope for a future is to find husbands where they came from.

For women of that era and culture, options were few. Finding a husband *might* (or might not) rescue them from economic and social disaster. Naomi has nothing for them. Being past the age of matrimony, she sees herself in an even direr predicament than they are. She doesn't want to bring them down with her. They should pursue whatever chances they might have at home. Her advice is sensible. Neither Ruth nor Orpah can come up with any response to contradict her.

At first, it looks as if Naomi may have won the argument. After another round of weeping, Orpah decides to go back to Moab. She kisses her mother-in-law goodbye. It's the right thing to do. The story itself hints at no criticism against Orpah for making this decision. Naomi has not only allowed it but insisted on it.

From any sensible perspective, Ruth should follow Orpah's example, but instead, she clings to Naomi. Contrasting Orpah and Ruth does not make Orpah look bad, but it does accentuate just how bold Ruth's decision is. As Trible puts it, "No God has called her; no deity has promised her blessing; no human being has come to her aid. She lives and chooses without a support group, and she knows that the fruit of her decision may well be the emptiness of rejection, indeed of death. Consequently, not even Abraham's leap of faith surpasses this decision of Ruth's."[5]

What was Ruth getting herself into? Between verses 8 and 15 of that chapter, Naomi warns her three times that she should go back to Moab, and she offers solid arguments each time. Ruth doesn't even bother to respond to those points. She shows no sign of hesitation and no signs that she is weighing the cost or considering the short-term and long-term risks. Her determination is firm. "Don't urge me to leave you or to turn back from you," she insists. "Where you go I will go, and where you stay I will stay. Your people will be my people and your God my God. Where you die I will die, and there I will be buried. May the LORD deal with me, be it ever so severely, if even death separates you and me" (vv. 16-17).

Biblical scholar James McKeown points out that "Ruth's decision is surprising because there was no obvious advantage in following Naomi. Her mother-in-law was not wealthy, and her tragic circumstances were weighing heavily on her. She was overcome with grief, and being in her company would be demanding and stressful."[6] Beyond Ruth's declaration of devotion to Naomi, she also commits to following Naomi's God. It is an extraordinary commitment without any hedging or equivocating. It is too much for Naomi to keep fighting against. She stops urging her daughter-in-law to leave her, and the two women continue the journey to Bethlehem.

A Bitter Arrival, Followed by a Plan and Hope

Naomi's homecoming is far from a happy occasion. Although her arrival causes a stir in the town, Naomi quickly extinguishes the celebratory mood by telling them not to call her Naomi. She tells them to call her "Mara," or "Bitter," "because the Almighty has made my life very bitter. I went away full, but the LORD has brought me back empty. Why call me Naomi [which means "Pleasant"]? The LORD has afflicted me; the Almighty has brought misfortune upon me" (Ruth 1:20-21). This pessimistic declaration echoes Naomi's earlier statement to Orpah and Ruth that "the LORD's hand has turned against me!" (v. 13). Naomi has convinced herself not simply that God has abandoned her or neglected her but also that he is actively working against her. This is part of the reason she didn't want her daughters-in-law to accompany her. She wanted to spare them the consequences of God's animus against her.

Naomi is far from alone in feeling this way. The book of Psalms, among other places in Scripture, is full of such outcries against God. Many people today have faced difficulties so enormous that it feels as if God must be deliberately working against them. Naomi's despair—her sense of being utterly alone—may have even motivated Ruth to stick with her mother-in-law so that she would at least have one person on her side.

Naomi tells the townspeople that the Lord has brought her back empty, but that isn't true. She has Ruth! Naomi makes no mention of this faithful daughter-in-law during her bitter homecoming remarks, but we know that Ruth is about to become the instrument of Naomi's rescue. God has not turned against Naomi. He is working behind the scenes in ways she never could have imagined to position her not only for happiness but also for a place in history.

There is a Cinderella element to this story. Is that one reason for its popularity? The hopelessness, the seeming impossibility of a good outcome, followed by the answer that no one could have seen coming? The good young Cinderella/Ruth saved by love, by the kinsman-redeemer prince/Boaz? If there is hope even for someone as bitter and despairing as Naomi and as seemingly powerless and overlooked as Ruth, then is there hope for us readers too? In that sense, this story asks some of the biggest questions of life: Who will rescue us? Who will acknowledge our plight? Who will redeem us?

Ruth and Naomi are about to find out, but their fortunes begin to shift in the most humble manner imaginable. Ruth tells Naomi, "Let me go to the fields and pick up the leftover grain behind anyone in whose eyes I find favor" (2:2). The women need to eat, and gleaning was a way this culture allowed the poor person and the stranger, both of which Ruth was, to gather enough provisions to survive.

Ruth picks a field at random, but her choice would change her life, Naomi's life, and ultimately the course of history through her offspring. The field she gleans belongs to Boaz. He happens to be a relative of Naomi, but Ruth doesn't know that. Why hadn't Boaz emerged in the story already to help his relative? And why didn't Naomi deliberately send Ruth to his field in order to seek his help? The text doesn't say. Ruth keeps her focus on one thing: gathering grain.

In the midst of her work, the boss shows up. Boaz greets the harvesters and asks the overseer to identify the new woman among them. The way Boaz asks about Ruth is significant. He says, "Who does that young woman belong to?" (v. 5). This question could be answered in a number of ways. She is the daughter-in-law of his relative Naomi. She is the widow of Mahlon. The overseer, however, answers, "She is the Moabite who came back from Moab with Naomi" (v. 6). This description of her only emphasizes her outsider status. She is a foreigner. She "came back" with Naomi, but their relationship is not mentioned. She also is obviously financially needy, or she wouldn't be gleaning, and besides that, she is a woman whose value lies in whom she "belongs to," which only adds to her vulnerability.

Boaz could respond in many ways to this stranger. He chooses to be protective and caring. He also reveals that even though he is meeting her for the first time, he already knows her by reputation, and he is favorably impressed. He tells her, "I've been told all about what you have done for your mother-in-law since the death of your husband—how you left your father and mother and your homeland and came to live with a people you did not know before. May the LORD repay you for what you have done. May you be richly rewarded by the LORD, the God of Israel, under whose wings you have come to take refuge" (vv. 11-12). Ruth's risky but loving decision to follow Naomi is now being validated. It does indeed look as if the Lord, the God of Israel, is taking Ruth under his wings, and Boaz acts quickly to bring her under his own protection also.

Boaz urges Ruth to glean only in his fields. He orders the men not to touch her. He orders his people to provide her water whenever she needs it and to help her glean by leaving stalks for her to pick up. He offers her food at mealtime. By the time the day is done and she has threshed the barley she gathered, she has many pounds of it to take back to Naomi.

One of the great things about the book of Ruth is how it shows what so many of us have experienced—the subtle but undeniable movement of the Holy Spirit into a situation that had seemed hopeless. Up to now, Ruth has not operated out of any carefully constructed long-term plan or clever scheme. She followed Naomi out of love, even though the cost to her own future looked enormous. She gleaned at a random field out of the need for survival. Was it chance alone that led her to just the right field, owned by just the right man? Was it mere coincidence that allowed Ruth—and her integrity—to be noticed by the one man willing and eager to turn her situation around? God's fingerprints are so apparent on these circumstances that even Naomi, Miss Bitter herself, who had declared herself "empty," cannot help but express hope once she hears what happened.

When Naomi finds out that Ruth had gleaned in Boaz's fields, she responds with an outburst of joy, saying that the Lord "has not stopped showing his kindness to the living and the dead" (v. 20). Is this really Naomi? From this point on in the story, given this hint of God's involvement and love, she moves from bitterness and hopelessness to action. Naomi tells Ruth that Boaz is a close relative and is one of their kinsmen-redeemers. According to Leviticus 25:25, such a redeemer had the responsibility to buy back family property for a family member who had been forced to sell it because of financial difficulties. Naomi now comes up with a plan. She makes up for her earlier pessimism and passivity with a bold plan that could easily backfire, not only on herself but particularly on Ruth.

From Hints of Hope to a Bold Plan of Action

Naomi is frank about her goal. She tells Ruth, "My daughter, I must find a home for you, where you will be well provided for" (Ruth 3:1). Marriage with Boaz isn't stated explicitly, but that is clearly what she has in mind. Her scheme for making that happen looks strange to modern eyes. Ruth is to show up that night at Boaz's threshing floor, wearing perfume and her best clothes. Once he has finished eating and drinking and lies down to sleep, she is to sneak over to where he is lying, uncover his feet, and lie there until he wakes up and tells her what to do. Commentators have probed the sexual innuendo or euphemistic phrasing of words such as "uncover his feet." Whatever their precise meaning, Ruth's actions with Boaz are daring and bold.

Ruth, who has not spent much time in this story agonizing or worrying about worst-case scenarios, agrees to follow Naomi's plan. She does everything Naomi tells her to do, and in the middle of the night, Boaz wakes up to find this young woman lying at his feet. This is where the story might have taken a very bad turn. Boaz could feel entrapped, startled, and insulted. He could accuse her of being scheming and manipulative. He could toss her out and make her life worse off than it has ever been.

He does none of those things. Instead, he compliments her for her noble character and for not running after the younger men. He acknowledges that he is a kinsman-redeemer, but there is one complication. There is another kinsman who is a closer relative and has to be given the chance to redeem the property that Naomi's husband had owned. The laws did not allow for land to simply be sold on the open market. The kinsman-redeemer would keep the land within the family. This sale would help give Naomi financial security.

Now it is time for Boaz to put a plan into action. In the meantime, he sends Ruth back secretly early in the morning, and he gives her a large gift of barley to take back to Naomi. Boaz acts quickly. That morning, he sets up a meeting between himself and the closer relative at the town gate. Ten elders are there as witnesses. Boaz explains the situation and offers the relative the chance to redeem the land. The man agrees to redeem it.

Boaz, however, ties the buying of the land to marrying Ruth, and that changes the relative's mind. He bows out of the deal, which allows Boaz to announce to everyone gathered, "Today you are witnesses that I have bought from Naomi all the property of Elimelek, Kilion and Mahlon. I have also acquired Ruth the Moabite, Mahlon's widow, as my wife, in order to maintain the name of the dead with his property, so that his name will not disappear from among his family or from his hometown. Today you are witnesses!" (4:9-10).

Notice how the happy ending of this story is worded in Ruth 4:13: "So Boaz took Ruth and she became his wife. When he made love to her, the

LORD enabled her to conceive, and she gave birth to a son." Ruth does not simply give birth to a son. She gives birth to a son *the LORD enabled her to conceive.* Even though Ruth and especially Naomi may have believed at the beginning of the story that God was absent or even hostile to them, in the end, his direct involvement is unmistakable. The ending is happy not only for Ruth but also for Naomi. The women rejoice with her over the intervention of the kinsman-redeemer and the birth of the child.

The story will also have a profound impact on the history of Israel and will extend to all humanity. As the final verses show, the name of Ruth's child is Obed, who will become the father of Jesse, who will become the father of David. That's as far as the genealogy takes it in the book of Ruth, but as Christians know, that line will eventually lead to Jesus.

The book of Ruth speaks to history, but it also speaks to us as ordinary individuals. As McKeown writes, the message of this story "is one of reassurance that when we are tempted like Naomi to feel forsaken by God, to feel that he does not care, he is nevertheless in control and will work out his purposes. This book encourages its readers not to panic during the dark times when God seems far away but to wait expectantly and to keep faith in him."[7]

Ruth and Naomi Inspire Artists and Musicians

The book of Ruth contains so many vivid moments that artists and musicians have found themselves captivated by very different aspects of it. Poet and artist William Blake depicted the story in his 1795 painting *Naomi and Ruth,* which shows Orpah, bent over and wiping away tears, moving away from her mother-in-law, Naomi. Ruth, wearing a similar white robe and bent over in a way that mirrors Orpah's posture, faces the opposite direction and is clinging to a dark-robed Naomi. The mother-in-law does not embrace Ruth but instead stands with her hands out, empty palms facing outward, as if to show she has nothing to offer her daughters-in-law.[8]

When Michelangelo painted Ruth on one of the arches in the Sistine Chapel in Vatican City in the early 1500s, he focused on a much happier moment. Ruth cuddles the sleeping baby Obed, holding him close to her as she closes her own eyes in a scene of deep contentment for mother and child.

Rembrandt's drawing of the Ruth story depicts a scene in which Boaz pours six measures of barley from a basket into Ruth's veil, which is spread on the ground in front of her and which she holds by two corners. Neither of them looks at the other, but each focuses instead on Boaz's generous gift as it pours out into the veil.[9]

Twentieth-century artist Marc Chagall created a series of paintings on the book of Ruth. One of the most moving ones shows Naomi flanked by Ruth and Orpah, the bodies of three women so close together that they almost seem to meld into one another. All three women wear expressions of grief, and both daughters-in-law touch Naomi with hands of comfort.[10]

Musicians also have retold the Ruth story. One of the most vivid encounters I have had with the book of Ruth was hearing a song cycle written by a singer/songwriter who is a friend of mine, Lynn Maudlin. Her musical is called *House of Bread*, which is the meaning of the word Bethlehem, Naomi's hometown. This musical, performed by five singers, powerfully brings out the human elements of the story—the uncertainty, the bitterness, the love, the promise. It emphasizes that this is a story of ordinary people trying to find their way through life, trying to understand God's ways, and making the best of the harsh reality that has been handed to them.

One of Naomi's songs, "I Am Bitter," speaks of how hard it is for her to continue living in the aftermath of the deaths of her husband and sons, as she prepares to return to Bethlehem:

How do I find the strength to go on?
How do I find the strength to live?
The girls are weak but they think I'm strong.
But I've got nothing left to give.[11]

How many people can relate to this feeling that the demands of life require more strength than they could possibly manage? Naomi is bitter and hopeless, but she still has to find a way to make the long journey to what had once been her home.

In "The Gleaning Song," Naomi describes the gleaning customs and laws to Ruth—that the corners of fields are left unharvested as a way of taking care of orphans and widows, who can glean them. Ruth says the men of this land are good for providing in this way, but Naomi responds,

Our law comes from God, not man
For God has pity on His people and provides for us—
But then she adds,
So why did He take away my provision?

Elimelech.
Ruth answers,
　Mahlon—
And both sing,
　And Chilion—
The final line of the song is Ruth singing,
　I will glean.[12]
Ruth accepts what God provides in the way he is willing to give it, which is not always the way she would prefer. One of the strange, hard truths of the book of Ruth is that God provides, but sometimes in such strange ways that it either doesn't look like provision, or it at least takes a long time for that reality to emerge. Ruth accepts, trusts, and then acts.

The final song of *House of Bread*, called "God Is Good," says,
　Our broken lives He weaves into His purpose
　Our broken hearts give access to His plans.[13]
It is not from Naomi and Ruth's abundance that God does his work. If these women had lived the easy, uncomplicated lives they wanted, with husbands who outlived them in a land that never endured famine, we would never have heard of them. God's amazing rescue is what makes their story worth telling. It's a reminder that in our own darkest moments, he may be doing the work that we may look back to see was the most worthwhile.

The Ruth and Naomi story has been adapted for children in some books and films, but in some ways it is a harder story to retell than a more straightforward story such as David killing Goliath or Noah filling an ark with animals. How does a children's writer handle scenes such as Ruth sneaking off to Boaz's threshing floor in the middle of the night to uncover his feet and lie there until he wakes up? Or what's the best way to explain that Boaz is a kinsman-redeemer but that there is another closer relative who has the first right to redeem the land and perhaps marry Ruth?

Veggie Tales has created a version of the story for children, and its approach is to take some of the themes and characters of the biblical story and turn it into a Ruth-like fairy tale. It doesn't retell the story so much as it pays homage to it by borrowing elements such as the loyalty of a daughter-in-law to a mother-in-law, the love story between the outsider and the powerful man, the courage and cleverness of the Ruth-Naomi duo, and the unexpected happy ending that can result when God is working out his purposes.

The *Veggie Tales* story is called "Duke and the Great Pie War," a title that certainly doesn't immediately bring to mind the book of Ruth. Instead of Naomi and Ruth, we have Nona and Petunia. They have come to live in the land of Scone, Nona's homeland. Petunia, who had been married to Nona's son, is not accepted in Scone because she is from a rival kingdom, Rhubarb. People call her people Rhubarbarians, and they don't like them, especially in the aftermath of the Great Pie War between the two kingdoms. At the beginning of the story, Nona and Petunia are poor, eating "water soup with water sauce."

Nona schemes to introduce Petunia to her distant cousin, the powerful Duke Duke. He is infatuated. His servants don't like his attention to this Rhubarbarian, but the romance continues anyway. Duke wins her over through a series of contests, and all ends happily.[14]

The book of Ruth may not get as much attention as certain other stories in the Bible, but what can readers glean from it?

God works in unexpected ways. Naomi and Ruth never could have anticipated how their story would turn out. Even at their worst moments, God had not abandoned them, but they could know that only by faith, not by what they saw around them. This story also shows that we do not yet know the end of our story. Even when we die, our story is not over, as the genealogy of the book of Ruth shows. God may be working in ways that we won't know until eternity.

God works as we act. Surrendering to despair isn't what brought about the positive ending of this story. Naomi had to make that hard journey back to Bethlehem. Ruth had to go out and glean. Naomi had to send Ruth to Boaz's threshing floor. God was at work behind the scenes all along, but none of what he did would have happened if Naomi and Ruth had allowed despair to have the final word.

God uses ordinary people to accomplish his purposes. These women had little money or power. Maybe you, too, are not a king or queen, and maybe you have not seen God in a burning bush, and maybe you have not slain a giant. God may still choose to do something significant in your life, bringing about your rescue as you make a difference for others.

Notes

1. Philip Jenkins, *The New Faces of Christianity: Believing the Bible in the Global South* (New York: Oxford University Press, 2006), 79.

2. Jenkins, 79.

3. Jenkins, 29.

4. Phyllis Trible, *God and the Rhetoric of Sexuality* (Philadelphia: Fortress Press, 1978), 167-68.

5. Trible, 173.

6. James McKeown, *Ruth* (Grand Rapids: Eerdmans, 2015), 25.

7. McKeown, 69.

8. Elizabeth Fletcher, "Bible Paintings—Ruth, Naomi and Boaz," WomenintheBible.net, accessed February 15, 2020, http://www.womeninthebible.net/bible-paintings/ruth-naomi/.

9. Fletcher.

10. Fletcher.

11. Lynn Maudlin, "I Am Bitter," *House of Bread*, accessed April 27, 2021, http://www.ruthmusical.com/lyrics_iambitter.htm. Quoted with permission from Lynn Maudlin, © 2001 Moonbird Music. All rights reserved.

12. Lynn Maudlin, "The Gleaning Song," *House of Bread*, accessed April 27, 2021, http://www.ruthmusical.com/lyrics_gleaning.htm. Quoted with permission from Lynn Maudlin, © 2002 Moonbird Music. All rights reserved.

13. Lynn Maudlin, "God Is Good," *House of Bread*, accessed April 27, 2021, http://www.ruthmusical.com/lyrics_god-is-good.htm. Quoted with permission from Lynn Maudlin, © 2004, 2005 Moonbird Music. All rights reserved.

14. Tim Hodge, director, *Veggie Tales on TV*, season 1, episode 9, "Duke and the Great Pie War" (Nashville: Big Idea Entertainment, 2005), YouTube video, 53:10, posted by "Veggie Tales Full Episodes," January 10, 2017, https://www.youtube.com/watch?v=pBEmjDldOWI.

Digging Deeper

1. Ruth 1:20-21 says, "'Don't call me Naomi [Pleasant],' she told them. 'Call me Mara [Bitter], because the Almighty has made my life very bitter. I went away full, but the LORD has brought me back empty. . . . The LORD has afflicted me; the Almighty has brought misfortune upon me.'" On arriving in Bethlehem, Naomi declares herself "Bitter" and believes that God not only has abandoned her but also is undermining her. Have you ever felt this way? Why is Naomi so bitter? In what ways is she justified? What is she overlooking in her despair? Is her situation as hopeless as she thinks?

2. The book of Ruth can be seen as a story about the way God moves into a hopeless situation and causes it to work out well. Do you agree with that interpretation? What other biblical stories also follow that pattern? Can you think of a situation in which that has happened in your own life?

3. This chapter discusses various scenes from the book of Ruth that have inspired painters and musicians. If you were to paint a scene from the book of Ruth, what scene would you choose? How would you depict it? Why does that scene stand out to you more than others?

Go to https://www.thefoundrypublishing.com/8OT/LeaderGuide for a free downloadable leader's guide that includes more questions for reflection as well as activities for use in a small group setting.

6

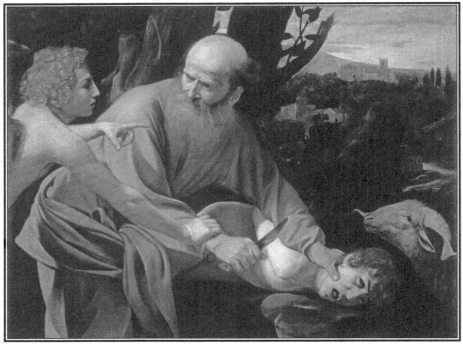

The Sacrifice of Isaac // Caravaggio // c. 1603-4

Abraham—
a Legacy as Vast as the Stars

[9] *When they reached the place God had told him about, Abraham built an altar there and arranged the wood on it. He bound his son Isaac and laid him on the altar, on top of the wood.* [10] *Then he reached out his hand and took the knife to slay his son.* [11] *But the angel of the LORD called out to him from heaven, "Abraham! Abraham!"*

"Here I am," he replied.

[12] *"Do not lay a hand on the boy," he said. "Do not do anything to him. Now I know that you fear God, because you have not withheld from me your son, your only son."*

[13] *Abraham looked up and there in a thicket he saw a ram caught by its horns. He went over and took the ram and sacrificed it as a burnt offering instead of his son.* [14] *So Abraham called that place The LORD Will Provide. And to this day it is said, "On the mountain of the LORD it will be provided."*

[15] *The angel of the LORD called to Abraham from heaven a second time* [16] *and said, "I swear by myself, declares the LORD, that because you have done this and have not withheld your son, your only son,* [17] *I will surely bless you and make your descendants as numerous as the stars in the sky and as the sand on the seashore. Your descendants will take possession of the cities of their enemies,* [18] *and through your offspring all nations on earth will be blessed, because you have obeyed me."*

—Genesis 22:9-18

ABRAHAM, like David and other great figures of the Bible, evokes many vivid pictures. What do you envision when you hear his name? Do you see him out in some vast wilderness, gazing up at the blazing stars as God promises him, improbably, that his descendants will be just as numerous as those shimmering lights? Do you see him listening to his ninety-year-old wife as she tells him that despite the years of desperate waiting and despite her earlier laughter at the idea, she is in fact pregnant? Do you see him negotiating with God to prevent the destruction of the cities of Sodom and Gomorrah?

Those are important Abrahamic moments, and Scripture records many others, but when I hear the name "Abraham," I picture only one scene: Abraham stands, knife in hand, over his beloved son Isaac, who lies bound to an altar covered with wood that Abraham will set ablaze as soon as he has completed the slaughter of the boy, whose neck is only inches from that knife blade and whose life is only seconds from ending.

How could such a story exist about a man who would one day tower over three faiths—Judaism, Christianity, and Islam—that encompass billions of people across the globe? Each of these religions claim Abraham as a central figure, and each believes that its own belief system is where Abraham's role and purpose are best fulfilled. How could such a major figure in world history even consider the possibility of slaughtering his innocent son? And how could the God with whom he has made a covenant order him to do it?

This chapter will look at the many ways Abraham has dominated those three major world religions, but first, I can't help but delve into this haunting story. Jews and Christians study the story as found in Genesis 22. Muslims study the variation found in the Qur'an. Many other versions exist outside those texts, and the stories have sparked countless commentaries from Jewish, Christian, and Muslim scholars over the centuries.

This story, which is called the Akedah in the Jewish tradition, retains its power because, like so much great literature, it is hard to simply read it and move on. It's a story that will keep rolling through your mind long after you have read it. It spawns questions not easily answered. Genesis 22 says that God was testing Abraham when he told him to take Isaac to the mountain and sacrifice him as a burnt offering. The question is, Was Abraham's response his most heroic act of faith, as some have seen it, or was it his biggest failure?

Did Abraham Fail the Test?

Renowned American attorney Alan M. Dershowitz, who is Jewish, wrote an admiring book on Abraham in which he observes that Abraham was not only the "world's first Jew" but also the "world's first lawyer." His successors are the "numerous Jewish lawyers who—for better or worse, but in my view mostly better—have changed the world by challenging the status quo, defending the unpopular, contributing to the rule of law, and following the biblical command to pursue justice."[1] Although Dershowitz believes Abraham behaved morally and brilliantly in other situations, when it comes to his willingness to sacrifice Isaac, Abraham turned into "a compliant fundamentalist who elevates dogma over reason, faith over morality. He willingly follows orders that will result in the death of the innocent, thereby becoming a Jew who is willing to sacrifice other Jews—indeed, his own flesh and blood—in order to remain in the good graces of an authority figure whom he fears."[2]

One earlier test that Dershowitz believes Abraham passed beautifully is when he uses his lawyer skills to challenge God's inclination to destroy the cities of Sodom and Gomorrah because of their wickedness. Abraham's nephew Lot is still living in Sodom, so Abraham hopes to save it from destruction. Abraham confronts the Lord and says, "Will you sweep away the righteous with the wicked? What if there are fifty righteous people in the city? Will you really sweep it away and not spare the place for the sake of the fifty righteous people in it? Far be it from you to do such a thing—to kill the righteous with the wicked, treating the righteous and the wicked alike. Far be it from you! Will not the Judge of all the earth do right?" (Genesis 18:23-25). God agrees that he would spare the city for that many righteous people. Then Abraham carefully negotiates with God to agree to spare the city if even forty-five righteous people can be found, then forty, then thirty, then twenty, then ten. The Lord agrees to all this.

Abraham has passed the test by standing up for the innocent, even though it meant courageously standing up to almighty God. So why would such a man not utter a single word of resistance when God says, "Take your son, your only son, whom you love—Isaac—and go to the region of Moriah. Sacrifice him there as a burnt offering on a mountain I will show you" (22:2)?

Abraham certainly has plenty of time to think of a response to God. This journey will take three days. Imagine the agony of this situation. To be a father, and to walk for three days with your beloved son, knowing that at the end of the journey you are going to kill him and watch his body burn. Conforming to the usual economy of biblical storytelling, the text gives no hint of what Abraham was thinking. It gives no sign that he had told Sarah or anyone else about God's command. How could he tell anyone? Whom could he have trusted not to stop him if they had known?

The idea of killing *any* son is horrific, but remember who Isaac is. From the earliest mention of Abraham in Genesis, when his name is still Abram (and Sarah's is Sarai) and God calls him out of Ur to move to a far-off land that is unknown to him, the Lord promises to make him a "great nation" through whom all the peoples on earth will be blessed (12:1-3). If that is to happen, Abraham will need a son, and that son is Isaac. And Isaac did not arrive easily. Abram and his wife Sarai were already old when God made this promise, and as the years went by, from a purely human standpoint, it looked less and less likely that it would be fulfilled.

Sarai eventually came up with her own plan for producing a son. She tells Abram to sleep with her servant Hagar in order to conceive a child. He does so, and a son named Ishmael is born. This complicated arrangement causes no end of trouble, but Ishmael is not the son God has in mind for fulfilling his covenant with Abram. God later tells Abraham (no longer named Abram) that Sarah herself (no longer named Sarai) will conceive a son named Isaac: "I will establish my covenant with him as an everlasting covenant for his descendants after him" (17:19). An everlasting covenant! Isaac is the key to the fulfillment of God's promises to Abraham. His very birth is a miracle. Abraham is one hundred years old and Sarah is ninety when he is born.

But now, Abraham trudges along on this three-day journey to sacrifice him. It's unthinkable. One day goes by. Two days. Three days. Abraham says nothing to God or Isaac or the servants or anyone. When they arrive at the spot God designates, Abraham makes Isaac carry the wood on which he will be sacrificed. Abraham carries the fire and the knife—sometimes translated "cleaver"—as the two of them prepare to carry out the deed. Isaac finally speaks up. "'The fire and wood are here,' Isaac said, 'but where is the lamb for the burnt offering?'" (22:7). Abraham assures him that God himself will provide the lamb for the burnt offering.

Abraham builds the altar. He places the wood. He binds his son. He places Isaac on top of the wood. So many questions this part of the story raises! Did Isaac resist? What terror flowed through him? Did Abraham waver? There is still time for Abraham to call a halt to this, to cry out to God, to walk away.

Islam has a different version of this sacrifice story. In the Qur'an, Abraham tells his son that he has seen in a dream that Abraham is to sacrifice him. The son, who is not specifically named in that part of the story, agrees to this: "He answered, 'O my father! Do as thou art bidden: thou wilt find me, if God so wills, among those who are patient in adversity!'" Some Muslim commentators have followed a tradition that the boy is Ishmael, not Isaac, since Islam places more emphasis on Ishmael than Isaac and presents the son of Abraham and Hagar as a model Muslim.[3]

But Genesis 22 speaks of no such awareness on Isaac's part. What he may have known or suspected or feared is left unstated. All we know is that everything is in place for his slaughter. The knife hovers above him. The torch burns nearby.

Then—finally—the angel of the Lord breaks in to stop the killing. The fact that this was a test is finally revealed to Abraham. "Now I know that you fear God, because you have not withheld from me your son, your only son," the angel says (22:12), and Abraham looks up to see a ram to sacrifice instead. Abraham's reward for passing this test, as the Lord had indicated before, is that he will be blessed. His descendants will be "as numerous as the stars in the sky and the sand on the seashore," and all nations will be blessed through his descendants (vv. 17-18).

Happy ending, right? Dershowitz doesn't see it that way. He asks, "How can one reconcile the confrontational and argumentative Abraham of the Sodom story with the compliant and acquiescing Abraham of the Akedah? . . . Why did he not accuse God of profanity in sweeping away yet another innocent . . . ? Can this compliant Abraham really be the same man who passed the Sodom test?"[4]

Those questions have vexed readers for centuries, but other commentators, such as philosopher Søren Kierkegaard and the writer of the New Testament book of Hebrews, have found courage and almost unimaginable faith where Dershowitz sees only passivity.

God Tests Abraham, but Is Abraham Testing God?

I certainly understand Alan Dershowitz's objection to Abraham's silence in the face of God's order to slaughter and sacrifice Isaac as a burnt offering. As a father myself, I can't help but think that my own first response would be outrage at such a command, quickly followed by confusion and fear. How could God *do* this?

Yet as I mentioned earlier, part of the greatness of this story is that it's hard to settle on a response to it. It keeps playing in your mind. You can't leave it alone. Dershowitz the lawyer likes Abraham best when Abraham is behaving like a lawyer. But was Abraham's challenge of God in the Sodom and Gomorrah incident really more impressive—more of a "passing of a test"—than his behavior in the near-sacrifice of Isaac?

When Abraham "negotiates" with God over how many righteous people it would take to save the two cities—persuading God from fifty, down to forty-five, and so on, all the way to ten—the Lord was no doubt pleased with Abraham's willingness to stand up for innocent life. However, Abraham's arguments were solid but not especially brilliant or original, certainly not anything God Almighty hadn't thought of himself already. God may have been satisfied that Abraham passed that test, if that is what it was, but Abraham did so without needing to show any *faith* in God or to step out on much of a limb intellectually or spiritually.

But the Isaac episode demanded an unprecedented show of faith and obedience. God wasn't simply telling Abraham his intention toward others, as in the Sodom and Gomorrah situation. Instead, he was telling Abraham to *do* something. It was a command that required an almost unthinkable degree of *trust* and commitment on Abraham's part, surely a bigger test than merely coming up with a lawyerly argument about God's intended actions.

God had much at stake in what happened with Isaac. This son was at the core of the relationship between God and Abraham. It had required years of trust on the part of Abraham and Sarah to keep believing that Isaac would even come. Would Abraham now trust God to do the impossible again with whatever this "offering" was about?

Elie Wiesel, a Nobel Peace Prize winner, Holocaust survivor, and Jewish writer, draws on the midrash, ancient rabbinic commentaries on Scripture, in his understanding of Abraham's actions. He offers the possibility that this is a "double-edged test." God is testing Abraham, but Abraham is also testing God. It's as if Abraham had said, "I defy You, Lord. I shall submit to Your will, but let us see whether You shall go to the end, whether You shall remain passive and remain silent when the life of my son—who is also Your son—is at stake!"[5] God is the one who relents at the end of the story. He calls off the sacrifice. Abraham had won. Wiesel writes that Abraham is "charitable" with God by not speaking up and accusing him and pointing out how God's order contradicted his promises. Just as in the other tests that Abraham passes, this one brings God and Abraham closer together.

Trusting God to Do the Impossible

Almost two hundred years before Alan Dershowitz and Elie Wiesel wrote about Abraham and Isaac, another influential thinker, Søren Kierkegaard, confronted this story in his classic work *Fear and Trembling*. His conclusions about Abraham's actions are starkly different. Dershowitz sees Abraham's response to God's command as a failure, but Kierkegaard sees it as an ideal example of faith.

What is so great about Abraham's faith? As Kierkegaard explains, Abraham is willing to go a step beyond where most of us are willing to venture. He is willing to move beyond any human calculation that could possibly show how this situation God has placed him in could turn out well. It is impossible from any rational perspective. Dershowitz faults Abraham for not relying on his logical, lawyerly skills, but Kierkegaard praises him for moving beyond those. During the entire trip to the place of sacrifice, Abraham believed the impossible. He "believed that God would not demand Isaac of him, while he still was willing to sacrifice him if it was demanded. He believed by virtue of the absurd, for human calculation was out of the question, and it was indeed absurd that God, who demanded it of him, in the next instant would revoke the demand."[6]

Because of his unwavering faith in God, Abraham does not have to understand *how* God can make the impossible happen. He only has to obey. Although it seems, for many readers, bizarre that Abraham can make this three-day trip with Isaac without agonizing, hesitating, crying out to God, or simply disobeying, Kierkegaard believes that Abraham's faith makes this demeanor understandable. He writes, "He climbed the mountain, and even at the moment when the knife gleamed he believed—that God would not demand Isaac. He was no doubt surprised then at the outcome, but by a double movement he had regained his original condition and therefore received Isaac more joyfully than the first time."[7]

Abraham displayed this extraordinary faith not only in this most arduous test but also in his other actions, starting from the time God called him to leave everything familiar to go to a promised land he knew nothing about. Kierkegaard writes, "He left his worldly understanding behind and took faith with him; otherwise he undoubtedly would not have emigrated but surely would have thought it preposterous."[8]

Such radical faith is admirable, but it also carries dangers. If it is not directed by God and toward God—if it is practiced in the hands of someone who is only following his or her own impulses rather than obeying God's true command—then it could lead to actions such as those taken by terrorists who claim to be acting on God's command. Understandably, some commentators have worried about this application of Abraham's story. Kierkegaard was aware of the danger, too, and was careful to reject the kind of fanaticism that would use faith in a coercive way to bolster a political or sectarian agenda. As C. Stephen Evans describes Kierkegaard's view, the "genuine person of faith would never try to impose any views on others in a doctrinaire or manipulative way, much less employ violence to force others to conform to his or her way of thinking."[9]

The New Testament also holds up Abraham as an exemplar of faith, but for different reasons than Kierkegaard sets forth. Abraham is extolled in what is commonly called the "faith chapter" of the book of Hebrews, which lists the heroes of faith such as Abel, Enoch, Noah, Moses, and Rahab. Abraham is mentioned in two sections of this chapter. First, he is commended for following God's call to go to a place that would later be his inheritance, even though he didn't know where he was going. Sarah also lived by faith in believing God's promise that she would bear a son even after childbearing age (11:8-12).

Several verses later, the writer returns to Abraham and specifically mentions the sacrifice incident with Isaac as an example of Abraham's deep faith: "Abraham reasoned that God could even raise the dead, and so in a manner of speaking he did receive Isaac back from death" (v. 19). Even if the worst had happened and Isaac had died, Abraham would have trusted God to bring him back to life, the Hebrews writer asserts. No matter what, Abraham trusted God.

Many Christians also read the Abraham and Isaac story prophetically, as anticipating the sacrifice of Jesus Christ on the cross. Isaac is made to carry the wood on which he is to be sacrificed, just as Jesus is required to carry his cross on which he will be crucified. The beloved son Isaac is not sacrificed, but as Hebrews 11 points out, he is symbolically brought back from the dead. In the case of Jesus, the beloved Son of God *is* sacrificed and then resurrected from the dead in order to provide a way of salvation for all who receive him.

Abraham and Artists: Painting the Sacrifice of Isaac

Bruce Feiler, in his book *Abraham: A Journey to the Heart of Three Faiths*, writes that he is puzzled by the fact that Abraham "has hardly been a towering figure in the history of art and entertainment. There is no Michelangelo statue that everyone can envision, as there is of David; no indelibly outstretched fingers on the ceiling of the Sistine Chapel, as there are for Adam."[10] He points out that Moses has been depicted in the acclaimed film by Cecil B. DeMille (*The Ten Commandments*) and in the popular animated film produced by DreamWorks (*The Prince of Egypt*), Joseph has been celebrated in Andrew Lloyd Webber's blockbuster musical (*Joseph and the Amazing Technicolor Dreamcoat*), and Jesus has appeared in countless film and artistic portrayals. Where are the popular and artistically renowned works of art and film and literature about Abraham?

It's true that when you mention Abraham, fewer works of art or popular culture immediately come to mind than they do with some other biblical figures, but Abraham still has had a deep impact on various art forms over the centuries. Furthermore, his impact is spread widely across Judaism, Christianity, and Islam, whereas some of the other biblical figures are not as prominent in the art forms of all three faiths.

Colum Hourihane, in his book *Abraham in Medieval Christian, Islamic, and Jewish Art*, lists hundreds of artistic depictions of the "sacrifice of Isaac" episode in the medieval period alone, and that is only in Christian art, which is the book's main focus. He also lists nearly fifty examples of that incident shown in Islamic art of the period, and more than thirty examples from Jewish art. Artworks depicting other scenes from Abraham's life number in the thousands. So although Abraham's story has not lent itself to as many Hollywood treatments as some of the other heroes of the Bible, it has been a steady presence in the creative work of every generation for many centuries.

As Hourihane shows, depictions of the Abraham-Isaac sacrifice story appear repeatedly in frescoes on church walls, on altars, on plaques, on the bases of church crosses, on stained-glass windows, on various religious vessels and medallions, in biblical manuscripts and other religious books, in woodcuts, in pen drawings, in metal carvings, on floor mosaics, in carvings on sarcophagi, on church exteriors, on tapestries, and elsewhere.[11] Many Christians in the twelfth or thirteenth centuries might not have had the ability to read the story of Abraham's near-sacrifice of his son, nor would they have had access to Bibles in their own language even if they could read, but the story was all around them in their churches, and even above them and beneath their feet.

Many of these scenes in these works of art are simple. To bring the Isaac sacrifice story to the viewer's mind, the artist often needed just a few elements: the bearded Abraham, the knife in his hand, the boy Isaac on the altar, and the angel ready to stop the slaughter. Some show the angel holding on to Abraham's uplifted arm; some show the angel's hand on the knife or sword itself. Some show the ram nearby or Isaac clutching the wood.

Of all the artistic renderings of the Abraham-Isaac story from any era, perhaps the most famous—and one of the most haunting—is Caravaggio's 1602 painting *The Sacrifice of Isaac*. The viewer's eye is immediately drawn to the knife in Abraham's right hand—a hand that is headed toward the neck of Isaac, his mouth open and face filled with terror. Abraham holds down Isaac's head with his left hand. Abraham's face, however, is looking in the opposite direction, at the angel, who points toward the other side of the painting, where a ram's head is visible just above Isaac's head. The angel points with his left hand and restrains—just barely—Abraham's forearm with his right hand. The position of the knife, and Abraham's furrowed brow as he looks at the angel, makes it appear as if Abraham will cease his action reluctantly, if at all. He looks fully committed to following through on God's command.

The Abraham-Isaac scene is only one of many Abrahamic scenes that artists have brought to life. Other episodes these artists have favored include Abraham's blessing by Melchizedek, various scenes with Hagar, and scenes with Abraham and Sarah (getting married, leaving Egypt, receiving the promise of Isaac, etc.).

The "Bosom of Abraham": Rock My Soul in Painting and Song

The "bosom of Abraham" is another concept that arises in songs and paintings about him. If you mention that phrase to people today, what immediately springs to mind for many of them is the old African-American spiritual "Rock-a My Soul." There are several versions of the song, which has been performed by Elvis Presley; Louis Armstrong; the Mormon Tabernacle Choir; Peter, Paul and Mary; and many others. The version that many people know best is the one often sung by children in Sunday school and elsewhere. Its lyrics say,

Rock-a my soul in the bosom of Abraham (repeat three times).
Oh, rock-a my soul!

So high you can't get over it,
So low you can't get under it,
So wide you can't get 'round it.
You gotta go in at the door.[12]

Some versions substitute "him," meaning God, for "it," and some substitute "You must come in through the Lamb," or Jesus, for the last line. The idea is that Jesus is the only way into the bosom of Abraham, or heaven. No one can get past God any other way.

Other versions of "Rock-a My Soul," such as one Elvis Presley sang, make specific reference to Jesus's parable of the rich man and Lazarus, in Luke 16:19-31. In that parable, Jesus tells of a beggar named Lazarus who dies, and the angels carry him to the "bosom of Abraham" (see v. 22, KJV). It represents a place of rest, or a waiting place where the righteous go before judgment day.

The rich man, by contrast, who had lived a life of power (symbolized by his purple clothing) and luxury, and who had ignored Lazarus when the poor man had sat hungry at his gate while the dogs "licked his sores" (v. 20), now is in torment in Hades. He asks Father Abraham to send Lazarus to him to dip "his finger in water and cool his tongue" (v. 24), but Abraham denies this request. Between Lazarus in Abraham's bosom and the rich man's place of torment is a chasm too wide to cross. The rich man asks for Abraham to send Lazarus to his five brothers to warn them, but Abraham denies this request also, saying that those brothers already have the teachings of Moses and the Prophets, and if they won't listen to them, then they wouldn't repent even if someone came back from the dead to warn them.

The "bosom" of Abraham is often interpreted to mean, as the New International Version of the Bible translates it, "Abraham's side," as a child might lean against a parent's side for comfort, or as people who in Jesus's day dined in a reclining position might lean against others next to them. It is a comforting image and is often used to refer to the place where the righteous go after death. In some Jewish writings the phrase "bosom of Abraham, Isaac, and Jacob" is used, indicating that after death the righteous will go to a place where these patriarchs reside.

The "bosom of Abraham" concept is popular on the friezes of Gothic cathedrals, in paintings of the medieval and other eras, in stained-glass windows, frescoes, mosaics, statues, and elsewhere. In many of the medieval depictions, the bearded Abraham holds a sheet in front of him, and sitting in it are people representing the souls in paradise.[13] Although Abraham in the popular imagination is often a stern figure, old and white bearded and aloof, the "bosom of Abraham" image brings a warmer, more comforting image. Finding shelter in the bosom of Abraham represents rest, protection, and eternal reward.

For children who grew up attending Sunday school in the United States, another song that prominently features Abraham—and lots of motion—is "Father Abraham Had Many Sons." It begins,

> *Father Abraham had many sons*
> *Many sons had Father Abraham*
> *I am one of them and so are you*
> *So let's all praise the Lord.*
> *Right arm!*[14]

As the children sing "Right arm," they pump their right arm up and down and start the chorus again, this time adding "Right arm! Left arm!" and then both arms are moving. The chorus is repeated with the motions of the right leg, left leg, chin up, chin down, turn around, and sit down. As a kid, I loved all that movement, even though I had no idea what all that marching around had to do with Abraham or his sons. I'm still not sure exactly what the connection between the lyrics and the motions is, unless the little dance is a way for children to praise the Lord that they, too, are "sons," or children, of Abraham.

Abraham did, in fact, have many sons. The best-known are Isaac and Ishmael, but he also had six sons with Keturah, the wife he married after Sarah's death. The song, however, is referring not just to Abraham's biological sons but also to his spiritual offspring, and that is how the Christian Sunday school children can sing, "I am one of them and so are you." The song may be referring to New Testament passages such as Galatians 3:7-9, in which Paul writes, "Understand, then, that those who have faith are children of Abraham. Scripture foresaw that God would justify the Gentiles by faith, and announced the gospel in advance to Abraham: 'All nations will be blessed through you.' So those who rely on faith are blessed along with Abraham, the man of faith."

Spiritually speaking, Paul asserts, Christians are Abraham's children just as much as Paul's fellow Jews are. In that sense, Abraham does indeed have many offspring, since not only Jews and Christians but also Muslims consider him a "father." Although Abraham has had an influential presence in art and music and other realms of culture, it is his status in those three faiths that marks his most significant impact. It may be helpful to consider more specifically what he means to the followers of each of those faiths.

Abraham in Judaism

It is hard to overstate the importance of Abraham within Judaism. What makes him so important? God established a covenant with Abraham that would last through the generations. The covenant, which is presented in Genesis 15, 17, and 22, promised a number of crucial things.

The number of Abraham's offspring would be vast. God compares them to the number of stars in the sky and the sand on the seashore. This was no short-term covenant, and not one limited to one man alone or one generation alone. It would be fulfilled throughout the centuries, even up to the present. The Jewish people, who have spread across the world from Abraham's day until now, represent those stars and grains of sand.

That God made a *covenant* is crucial, because it was an agreement he would never back away from. As a quick read through the Old Testament will show, the generations after Abraham often disobeyed God. They fell away, were exiled, were scattered, or were enslaved, but God never gave up on them. He brought them back each time because of that crucial covenant with Abraham. Episodes from Abraham's own life—including the miraculous birth of Isaac to this old couple—showed that the later generations would have to be entirely dependent on God for their success. Only he could rescue them and bring them through the many disasters they would face, but so strong was his commitment to them that he would not let them go.

The covenant included land. The promised land, Canaan, Israel, would prove hard to get and hard to keep. But it was for Abraham and his descendants, and God would bring them into it. This was a promise that would transcend any particular generation.

God promised to make Abraham fruitful, the father of many nations. He promised that kings and nations would spring from Abraham, and this promise would be fulfilled through the birth of Isaac to Abraham and Sarah. Furthermore, God promised that all nations would be blessed through Abraham. This puts Abraham's descendants at the center of God's plan to save the entire world. They hold a special place in history and in God's plan. As Karl-Josef Kuschel puts it, "God has chosen for himself a people (one of the smallest and most insignificant peoples) to be a mediator of blessing for all peoples, as a way of becoming a God for all peoples, again out of pure grace, in full freedom."[15]

For the Jewish people, Abraham establishes their special relationship with God. They are connected to Abraham not only ideologically or spiritually but also physically, as actual descendants. Kuschel writes, "'Our Father Abraham'—that was the proud formula. To be the 'seed' of Abraham, the 'child' of Abraham: that was the all-important thing. Abraham our father, Moses, our teacher; around these poles, like an ellipse, life revolved for any pious Jew. And Abraham in particular was the idealized figure with which Jews faithful to the law identified."[16]

Abraham in Islam

One of the signs of how important Abraham, or Ibrahim, is in Islam is that he is mentioned in their five prayers every day. With all those millions of prayers taking place all over the world, Abraham is mentioned daily by more Muslims than by the people of any other faith. He plays many other important roles in Islam, such as the following:

- The Prophet Muhammad is said to descend from Abraham, through Ishmael.

- Abraham is mentioned in twenty-five suras, or chapters, of the Qur'an, second only to Moses. One sura is named for him.

- Abraham and Ishmael are said to have built the Kaaba, the sanctuary in Mecca, the most holy site in Islam. Muslims are to pray facing toward it, no matter where in the world they may be. Every Muslim, if possible, is supposed to make a pilgrimage to it at least once in a lifetime, a pilgrimage initiated by Abraham.

- Versions of many of the stories about Abraham from Genesis are told in the Qur'an.

- The Qur'an extols Abraham as an ideal believer. As Brannon Wheeler explains, "In the Qur'an, God calls upon people to 'follow the religion of Abraham' (Qur'an 3:95). Abraham is the 'model' of obedience to God (Qur'an 16:120) and the 'friend of God,' and no one can be 'better in religion' (Qur'an 4:125) than those who follow him."[17]

Abraham in Christianity

Readers of the New Testament will have no difficulty figuring out whether Abraham plays a significant role in Christianity. He is right there in the first verse of the first book: "This is the genealogy of Jesus the Messiah the son of David, the son of Abraham" (Matthew 1:1).

Mary, Zechariah, John the Baptist, Jesus, Paul, and other New Testament figures bring Abraham into their messages repeatedly. For Jews in particular, the physical descent from Abraham was the crucial element that made them children of Abraham, but followers of Christ see themselves as children of Abraham for a different reason: they are in his lineage of *faith*. As Paul argues forcefully in Galatians, Christ is the fulfillment of the promises God made to Abraham: "He redeemed us in order that the blessing given to Abraham might come to the Gentiles through Christ Jesus, so that by faith we might receive the promise of the Spirit" (3:14). Later in that chapter, he writes, "If you belong to Christ, then you are Abraham's seed, and heirs according to the promise" (v. 29).

In Romans 4, Paul emphasizes that Abraham was justified not through works, but instead through faith: "What does Scripture say? 'Abraham believed God, and it was credited to him as righteousness'" (v. 3). He later adds, "The words 'it was credited to him' were written not for him alone, but also for us, to whom God will credit righteousness—for us who believe in him who raised Jesus our Lord from the dead. He was delivered over to death for our sins and was raised to life for our justification" (vv. 23-25).

Christians look to Abraham as an exemplar of faith. Christ is the ultimate fulfillment of God's promises to Abraham, and salvation through Christ is available to everyone, not only Abraham's physical descendants.

Why Abraham?

What was so special about Abraham that he should be such a dominant figure in the faiths of billions of people and be so blessed by God? Nothing outward. He was a simple man. Without God's call and intervention, he no doubt would have lived a very ordinary life and would have died and been forgotten. You can say that about many major figures in the Bible. What was so special about Mary or Moses or Ruth or Jesus's disciples or even David, the youngest and most overlooked brother?

I love that God calls and blesses ordinary people. We don't need to earn his love with amazing skills or good looks or worldly credentials. Abraham wasn't extraordinary in human terms. God could have found a thousand just like him out there in the desert. If anything sets Abraham apart, it is his faith. As the "sacrifice of Isaac" story shows, he was simply all-in when it came to trusting God. He was not afraid to challenge God, but he also trusted the Lord even when a solution looked impossible. No matter what else may be said of him, that alone makes Abraham worth celebrating.

Notes

1. Alan M. Dershowitz, *Abraham: The World's First (but Certainly Not Last) Jewish Lawyer* (New York: Schocken Books, 2015), xi.

2. Dershowitz, xiii.

3. Karl-Josef Kuschel, *Abraham: Sign of Hope for Jews, Christians and Muslims* (New York: Continuum, 1995), 155.

4. Dershowitz, *Abraham*, 29.

5. Elie Wiesel, *Messengers of God: Biblical Portraits and Legends* (New York: Random House, 1976), 81.

6. Søren Kierkegaard, *Fear and Trembling*, ed. C. Stephen Evans and Sylvia Walsh, trans. Sylvia Walsh (Cambridge, UK: Cambridge University Press, 2006), 29.

7. Kierkegaard, 29.

8. Kierkegaard, 14.

9. C. Stephen Evans, introduction to *Fear and Trembling*, by Søren Kierkegaard, ed. C. Stephen Evans and Sylvia Walsh, trans. Sylvia Walsh (Cambridge, UK: Cambridge University Press, 2006), xxvi.

10. Bruce Feiler, *Abraham: A Journey to the Heart of Three Faiths* (New York: Harper Perennial, 2005), 69-70.

11. Colum Hourihane, ed., *Abraham in Medieval Christian, Islamic and Jewish Art* (University Park, PA: Pennsylvania State University Press, 2013), 106-61.

12. "Rock-a My Soul," Making Music Fun, accessed May 20, 2021, https://www.makingmusicfun.net/htm/f_mmf_music_library_songbook/rocka-my-soul-lyrics.php.

13. Hourihane, *Abraham*, 86-87, 90-92, 96-102.

14. "Father Abraham," Kididdles.com, accessed June 1, 2021, https://www.kididdles.com/lyrics/f033.html.

15. Kuschel, *Abraham*, 23.

16. Kuschel, 69.

17. Brannon Wheeler, "Abraham and Islam," Bible Odyssey, accessed on November 2, 2018, https://www.bibleodyssey.org/en/people/related-articles/abraham-and-islam.

Digging Deeper

1. Attorney Alan M. Dershowitz, who analyzes Abraham as "the first Jewish lawyer," argues that Abraham should have challenged God when the Lord commanded Abraham to sacrifice Isaac, just as Abraham had challenged God in earlier situations. Review what Dershowitz says. Do you agree, or is there a better way to interpret Abraham's obedience?

2. This chapter points out that although Abraham is a revered figure across the world and is key to the Jewish, Christian, and Islamic faiths, he has not attained the appeal in popular culture that some other biblical figures have enjoyed. Moses, Noah, and David, for example, have all been portrayed in popular movies. But what about Abraham? Why do you think his dramatic story has not been retold similarly? Do you think artists and filmmakers of our day will eventually pay more attention to Abraham?

3. Abraham's story is a crucial part of the Old Testament, but he also shows up in a number of places in the New Testament. Jesus, Paul, Mary, Zechariah, and John the Baptist all refer to him. One of the prominent places where Abraham is discussed is in the "faith chapter," Hebrews 11. Review what that chapter says about him. What aspects of Abraham's faith does it emphasize? What can we learn from those elements of faith to put into practice in our own lives?

Go to https://www.thefoundrypublishing.com/8OT/LeaderGuide for a free downloadable leader's guide that includes more questions for reflection as well as activities for use in a small group setting.

7

Shepherd herding sheep in Judean Hills near Jericho // Nathan Benn

Psalm 23—
Trusting the Shepherd

A psalm of David.

¹ *The* LORD *is my shepherd, I lack nothing.*
²   *He makes me lie down in green pastures,*
  he leads me beside quiet waters,
³   *he refreshes my soul.*
He guides me along the right paths
    for his name's sake.
⁴ *Even though I walk*
    through the darkest valley,
I will fear no evil,
    for you are with me;
your rod and your staff,
    they comfort me.
⁵ *You prepare a table before me*
    in the presence of my enemies.
You anoint my head with oil;
    my cup overflows.
⁶ *Surely your goodness and love will follow me*
    all the days of my life,
and I will dwell in the house of the LORD
    forever.

—Psalm 23

EVEN IF you could not identify any other psalm, you probably still are able to recognize Psalm 23. It is the passage of choice for countless funeral programs, church bulletins, inspirational posters, and bookmarks and just about any other object on which words can be printed. You may have heard snippets of it recited in so many sermons, television shows, and movies (*Titanic, X-Men, Pale Rider,* and others) that you may be able to recite much or all of it even if you never deliberately tried to memorize it. It's only six verses long, but almost every phrase in it has become famous in its own right, especially in the King James Version: "the valley of the shadow of death" (v. 4), "thy rod and thy staff they comfort me" (v. 4), "my cup runneth over" (v. 5), "he leadeth me beside the still waters" (v. 2), and the opening line, which has become a kind of title, "The LORD is my shepherd" (v. 1).

Though attributed to the giant-killing warrior King David, this psalm draws on imagery from one of his very different roles, that of a shepherd.

For centuries readers have found comfort in its portrayal of God as a generous, loving shepherd watching over his flock.

If you want the words of this psalm hovering over you, one company sells a wall decal that you can hang next to your bed. If you want to wear the psalm, you can buy a T-shirt that says, "The Lord is my Shepherd. I shall not want." You can buy a psalm app for your electronic devices, or how about a framed poster that says, "I will not be afraid because you are with me"? You can remind yourself of individual verses from the psalm with engraved bracelets, an engraved wind chime, a Psalm 23:4 dog tag, or a throw rug with the entire psalm displayed. You can even buy a pocketknife with Psalm 23 carved into the blade.

"Psalm" means song, so if you want to hear Psalm 23 sung, you have many recordings to choose from, since this psalm has been set to music in countless ways in every musical style imaginable. You can hear it in recordings of children's choirs, adult choirs, worship bands, and contemporary artists. Some put music to the words of the psalm itself, while others create their own songs from the well-known phrases and ideas of the poem. Musicians as diverse as Pink Floyd, U2, Kanye West, and Megadeth have included references to Psalm 23 in their works.

Maybe instead of singing the psalm, you want to read what prominent writers have to say about it. Best-selling authors such as Max Lucado, Beth Moore, Harold S. Kushner, and Robert J. Morgan have written books about this one short psalm. Many scholars have analyzed the psalm in biblical commentaries, and other writers have produced Bible studies, devotionals, and a prayer journal about the psalm. You can even buy a coloring book for adults that features phrases from the psalm surrounded by floral patterns. Dr. Ken Curtis created a video called *Reflections on Psalm 23 for People with Cancer.* One novelist, Debbie Viguié, has written a series of mysteries called the Psalm 23 Series, featuring books with titles such as *A Table Before Me, In the Presence of Mine Enemies,* and *Thy Rod and Thy Staff.*

What about All Those Other Psalms?

Psalm 23 is only one of 150 psalms in the Bible. The influence of the book of Psalms is incalculable. C. S. Lewis, N. T. Wright, Walter Brueggemann, Dietrich Bonhoeffer, Gordon J. Wenham, Eugene H. Peterson, and many others have written influential books about the psalms. The psalms have moved people because they touch on almost every emotion and spiritual question imaginable. They embody praise, lament, history, and theology. They express love, hate, joy, anger, and frustration.

How influential have the psalms been? Consider one example from the seventeenth century. The books a culture chooses to publish reveal much about what that culture values. The first book printed in English in the British colonies in North America, even before the Bible itself, was a new edition of the book of Psalms. *The Bay Psalm Book* was printed in 1640 in Massachusetts on a printing press brought there from England. It's not that these Puritans didn't already have various English translations of the book of Psalms available to them. In addition to the book of Psalms in the Bible itself, there were also versions such as the one in the Book of Common Prayer that was used for devotional worship and others that were translated into metrical versions for singing in church. Thomas Sternhold had translated the book of Psalms into a popular metrical version that could be sung, and *The Bay Psalm Book* was also used for that purpose. As Bible historian Lori Anne Ferrell explains, "By the early seventeenth century, in fact, many Bibles were bound with the Prayer Book, which contained a full copy of the Coverdale Psalms, *and* a copy of Sternhold, which meant that the folk who possessed a Bible 'fully loaded' would own the Psalms in three forms: as scripture, as worship, and as song."[1]

The psalms were already many centuries old by the time the Puritans translated them, of course, and even in ancient Israel they had been used for a variety of purposes—as prayers, as songs sung in the temple, and for use in private worship. They took hundreds of years to collect. They were written over a period of nearly eight hundred years, from the time of Moses to the third or second century B.C.[2] Jews and Christians of every denomination and category have sung, read, contemplated, and translated these poems for the past three thousand years. As commentator Gerald H. Wilson puts it, when you speak the psalms today, you speak words that have been spoken millions of times before in countless languages across the world. Furthermore, "as you read or sing or pray, off to your right stand Moses and Miriam, in front of you David and Solomon kneel down, to your left are Jesus, Peter and Paul, Priscilla and Aquila, while from behind come the voices of Jerome, St. Augustine, Theresa of Avila, Luther, Calvin, and more—so many more!"[3]

The historical details of how the psalms were first used in ancient Israel are sketchy, but clues within the psalms themselves indicate they were used within worship in the First Temple (Solomon's Temple), which was destroyed in 586 B.C. The headings of twenty-four psalms contain the names of guilds of temple singers, such as the Sons of Korah. These and other names, as Wilson points out, "so clearly associated with the official organization of the musical worship of the Jerusalem temple adds weight to the view that many of the psalms originated as public performance pieces produced by groups of singers with official oversight of the temple service."[4]

Some psalms include musical instruction—which instruments should be used or what tune a psalm should be sung to. Or they say "to the director" or give other indications of their use in worship. Some include specific functions for which the psalm should be used, such as "for the thank offering" in Psalm 100 (RSV). Sometimes as I read the psalms today, so many centuries after their first use, I try to imagine the lyres, cymbals, drums, and the voices of the singers who intoned these words for the worshippers so long ago.

Just as the psalms have been a crucial part of Jewish worship since ancient times, they have also been part of the Christian tradition since the time of Jesus and the early church. In Ephesians 5:18-20, Paul urges believers to "be filled with the Spirit, speaking to one another with psalms, hymns, and songs from the Spirit. Sing and make music from your heart to the Lord, always giving thanks to God the Father for everything, in the name of our Lord Jesus Christ." In Colossians 3:16, he urges the church to "teach and admonish one another with all wisdom through psalms, hymns, and songs from the Spirit, singing to God with gratitude in your hearts." According to Wilson,

> In the Christian New Testament, no book is cited more often as a warrant for understanding the life of Jesus than the book of Psalms. Particularly influential are Psalms 2 and 22, which mirror the two sides of Jesus that the church came to regard as key to understanding his work: his messianic sonship (Ps. 2) and his vicarious, sacrificial death (Ps. 22). But pride of place certainly goes to the messianic interpretations of Psalm 110, the most frequently cited psalm in the entire New Testament.[5]

The psalms have a prominent place within the worship and traditions of every branch of Christianity. As observed earlier, the Book of Common Prayer, which plays a key role in the practice of faith and worship in Anglican churches, includes all 150 psalms. In the Catholic tradition, the Liturgy of the Hours includes psalms for prayer at the various times of day and night. In many Protestant churches today, choruses and hymns based on psalms are included in almost every worship service, even if congregations who are singing them are sometimes unaware of the source of those lyrics.

The Book People Turn to in Joy, Sorrow, Despair, Celebration

But as important as the book of Psalms has been historically and in formal liturgy and public worship, it's not enough to think of it only in those realms. The book of Psalms is very *personal* to people, more so than probably any other book of the Old Testament. The book of Psalms is what people turn to when they're in distress and need comfort. When I think of the book of Psalms, the first image that comes to my mind is not of a congregation quietly listening to a reading of a psalm or a worship band leading their church in a psalm-inspired chorus. Instead, I picture a person alone, in distress, reaching out to God through these powerful ancient words.

Many people have favorite psalms that they turn to when the worst things happen. No matter how many times they have read the words before, they will go back to them again for reassurance and for connection with the Holy Spirit. Psalm 46 is one such favorite for many. It begins,

God is our refuge and strength,

an ever-present help in trouble.

Therefore we will not fear, though the earth give way

and the mountains fall into the heart of the sea,

though its waters roar and foam

and the mountains quake with their surging. (Vv. 1-3)

Or how about Psalm 27:1-3, which confidently declares,

The LORD is my light and my salvation—

whom shall I fear?

The LORD is the stronghold of my life—

of whom shall I be afraid?

When the wicked advance against me
    to devour me,
it is my enemies and my foes
    who will stumble and fall.
Though an army besiege me,
    my heart will not fear;
though war break out against me,
    even then I will be confident.

When I have faced tough times, one of my friends always points me to Psalm 91, which begins,

Whoever dwells in the shelter of the Most High
    will rest in the shadow of the Almighty.
I will say of the LORD, "He is my refuge and my fortress,
    my God, in whom I trust."

Surely he will save you
    from the fowler's snare
    and from the deadly pestilence.
He will cover you with his feathers,
    and under his wings you will find refuge;
    his faithfulness will be your shield and rampart. (Vv. 1-4)

Psalms can be comforting in bad times, but they also capture the joy of following the Lord like no other words in Scripture. Psalm 103:1-5 celebrates with the words,

Praise the LORD, my soul;
    all my inmost being, praise his holy name.
Praise the LORD, my soul,
    and forget not all his benefits—
who forgives all your sins
    and heals all your diseases,
who redeems your life from the pit
    and crowns you with love and compassion,
who satisfies your desires with good things
    so that your youth is renewed like the eagle's.

Given the praise emphasis of so many psalms, it's no wonder songwriters have mined these verses repeatedly for material for hymns and worship songs. A songwriter doesn't have to stretch too far to turn this into a worship chorus:

Give thanks to the LORD, for he is good.

His love endures forever.

Give thanks to the God of gods.

His love endures forever.

Give thanks to the Lord of lords:

His love endures forever.

to him who alone does great wonders,

His love endures forever. (136:1-4)

Psalms range from the height of praise to the depths of despair. Psalmists are not afraid to raise tough questions. They are not afraid to confront God or to pour out agony and a sense of dread and injustice. They are not always polite. The category that scholars call the psalms of lament—but which could also be called the psalms of outcry, complaint, or even horror—makes a place in Scripture for the most disturbing human emotions. In Psalm 31 the writer cries out,

My life is consumed by anguish

and my years by groaning;

my strength fails because of my affliction,

and my bones grow weak.

Because of all my enemies,

I am the utter contempt of my neighbors

and an object of dread to my closest friends—

those who see me on the street flee from me.

I am forgotten as though I were dead;

I have become like broken pottery. (Vv. 10-12)

Some of these psalms not only complain about the harsh circumstances of life, but they also target God himself:

Awake, Lord! Why do you sleep?

Rouse yourself! Do not reject us forever.

Why do you hide your face

and forget our misery and oppression?

We are brought down to the dust;

our bodies cling to the ground. (44:23-25)

Another psalm agonizes,

But I cry to you for help, LORD;

in the morning my prayer comes before you.

Why, LORD, do you reject me

and hide your face from me?

From my youth I have suffered and been close to death;

I have borne your terrors and am in despair.

Your wrath has swept over me;

your terrors have destroyed me. (88:13-16)

Given this harsh content, it might seem as if these psalms would be depressing, but for many readers, the impact is quite different. These psalms are liberating. They free the reader to know our relationship with God can absorb any emotion we throw at him. When we approach God, we do not have to get our act together first and pretend we have come to terms with our fears or our suffering or our devastating disappointments and losses. If we are angry, even at God, we can bring that to him.

What if our anger gets out of control and crosses into rage and a desire for revenge? Do we have to suppress that or hide it from God? Psalm 137:8-9 says,

Daughter Babylon, doomed to destruction,

happy is the one who repays you

according to what you have done to us.

Happy is the one who seizes your infants

and dashes them against the rocks.

Wow! Dashing the infants of enemies against the rocks? A horrifying thought, but some people who read this psalm may know exactly that depth of agony and bitterness. People do not have to hide those extreme emotions from God.

I once took a theology course in which we studied the psalms of lament and then were asked to write one of our own and then read it to the class. It was a gut-wrenching exercise, both in the writing and in the experience of reading and hearing all those psalms. Some people cried as they read their own psalms out loud, laying bare their grievances, sometimes for the first time in such an extended way. Some of their psalms focused on people who had hurt them. Others focused on tremendous losses they had endured—fractured relationships, the death of a child or spouse, betrayal by a business partner. These modern-day psalmists cried to God, just as the psalmists did thousands of years ago, and they looked to him for relief and rescue.

The psalms of lament are written from the perspective of a person or a community that is so deeply in relationship with the Lord that no matter how desperate the situation becomes, the psalmist is confident of God's eventual rescue. The psalmist can cry out to God without worrying that relationship will be broken. These psalms are intimate, even when they are angry or accusatory. Love and respect still are at the core of them.

In Psalm 31, for example, which speaks of a life beset with enemies and consumed by anguish and groaning, the psalmist still manages to affirm,

But I trust in you, LORD;
I say, "You are my God."
My times are in your hands;
deliver me from the hands of my enemies,
from those who pursue me. (Vv. 14-15)

The psalms deeply and dramatically reflect on many aspects of God—his power, his love, his wrath, his seeming aloofness at times, his creativity, his beauty, his determination to rescue his people. They also capture the many sides of a lifelong relationship with God—gratitude, bewilderment, love, awe, complaint, disappointment, surprise, confidence. The book of Psalms is a collection of poems, but it can be read almost as a journal, or collection of journals, that records the spiritual journeys of God's followers.

The Power and Influence of Psalm 23

With all that rich content, Psalms would remain one of the most beloved books of the Bible even if it did not include Psalm 23, but that one psalm still has captured the imagination of readers in ways that no other psalm can match. In the United States, one Christian leader who helped draw attention to this psalm was the popular preacher Henry Ward Beecher (1813-87), who wrote a tribute to it. Beecher wrote that God has sent this psalm "to speak in every language on the globe. It has charmed more griefs to rest than all the philosophy of the world. It has remanded to their dungeon more felon thoughts, more black doubts, more thieving sorrows, than there are sands on the seashore."[6] He writes in similar emotionally heightened language about how the psalm has consoled the sick, the captives, the widows, orphans, and slaves.

As comforting as Psalm 23 may be, however, it is not simply a sentimental poem filled with feel-good imagery. It is an exploration of the meaning of faith and a profound portrait of how a loving heavenly Father operates. It does not paint a false picture of an easy green-pasture world, where nothing bad happens. No, this place, like our own lives, has enemies. It has the "valley of the shadow of death" (v. 4, KJV). Why is the shepherd there in the first place? Not because life is easy, but because life is hard. The life of the sheep is full of danger, and only the shepherd can be trusted to keep the sheep from destruction. Psalm 23 presents a vision of a God in control, a loving shepherd who does not remove the sheep from the heartache-filled world but instead leads them *through* it.

This psalm shows as vividly as any other passage of the Bible the sheep's total dependence on the love of the Shepherd, or our total dependence on the love of the heavenly Father. We may have illusions of self-sufficiency, but the reality is we rely on him for every breath, and for the breath of life itself. Without him, we would be destroyed in an instant.

Our dependence is not servile or demeaning. He loves us. He cares for us. He is leading us ultimately to a good place. We can rest in him. We can take pleasure in the life he has given us despite the threats that surround us. We don't have to hide or grasp or beg. He already knows our needs. He sees dangers we're unaware of. Because our vision is so limited, we won't always understand what he's doing or why he's doing it. He cares about us so much that his love pursues us, even though it may not always feel that way. Blind to many of the dangers that surround us, we may fight him when he forces us out of our own blundering course. But over the long haul, we can learn that he is the source of the refreshment of our soul. He leads us to what is best. We can trust him. We can love him.

Psalm 23 uses that imagery of sheep and a shepherd. Those images would have been part of the everyday lives of most of the original hearers of this psalm. Today, most of us know about sheep and shepherds only secondhand, from stories and biblical passages. We can understand the broad outlines of these metaphors, but it's easy to miss the nuances of this imagery. One modern shepherd, W. Phillip Keller, wrote a book about Psalm 23 that has become a classic in its own right, with more than a million copies sold since it first came out in 1970. Keller understands the shepherd-sheep imagery from a variety of perspectives. He grew up in East Africa, where shepherds used practices that were similar to those in the Middle Eastern setting of the psalm. He also worked as a sheep owner and rancher for eight years. As a lay pastor, he shepherded a congregation of Christians.

A Shepherd Looks at Psalm 23 brings new understanding even to the lines in the psalm that seem the most straightforward. "He makes me to lie down in green pastures" (v. 2, NKJV) seems pretty clear. I picture a cute lamb lying down in a lush, green field, safe and content. However, it isn't that simple. Because of their vulnerability, sheep do not settle down easily. Keller says that before they are willing to lie down, sheep must be free of fear. They also must be free of friction from other sheep within the flock and free of torment by flies or parasites. They also must be free of hunger. Those are big demands. Who is the only one who can rid the sheep of all those threats and make them feel safe enough to lie down in green pastures? The good shepherd. Keller writes, "A flock that is restless, discontented, always agitated and disturbed never does well. And the same is true of people."[7]

Sheep have good reasons to be fearful. Keller reports that dogs have been known to slaughter as many as 292 sheep in one night. They have only the shepherd to rely on. Keller writes, "In the course of time I came to realize that nothing so quieted and reassured the sheep as to see me in the field. The presence of their master and owner and protector put them at ease as nothing else could do, and this applied day and night."[8] For people of faith, true contentment is found only in the Shepherd's presence, regardless of circumstances. Psalm 23 is a psalm of David. He was a powerful man—a king, a military leader, a giant killer. If anyone should be tempted toward self-reliance, it was David. But he was also a shepherd. He knew that, like sheep, human beings are also more vulnerable than they realize. David spent plenty of time being hunted, threatened, and punished. He knew that human power ultimately was not enough to save him. He sometimes fell short morally and in other ways. He could not save himself. Ultimately, he knew that his only true source of well-being was God his Shepherd.

"Green pastures" sound nice, and metaphorically, most of us might want to spend our lives in such pleasant and pastoral places. But another biblical scholar, Ray Vander Laan, shows that what the term "green pastures" meant to the original hearers of this psalm is very different from what it means to most of us today. Vander Laan narrates a video that is set in an area of the Negev wilderness called "green pastures." It looks entirely different from what that name conjures up. The land on which he stands is a rocky, hilly, brown, seemingly barren landscape. Where is the green? Where are the pastures?

Vander Laan explains that from biblical times to today, sheep have grazed in this wilderness rather than in more lush farming areas. Good farming land is scarce in that region of the world, so farmers do not want sheep grazing in it. Instead, the sheep are led across paths in this wilderness area. But what do they eat? The video shows sheep grazing, but from a distance, it looks as if they have only rocks for food. A closer look, however, shows that tufts of grass grow next to many of those rocks. This parched landscape gets a small amount of rain every year, and the air also holds some moisture from the breezes that come from the Mediterranean Sea. That moisture drips into the ground next to the rocks and allows for the growth of these precious blades of grass.[9]

This rocky landscape has implications for the spiritual meaning of Psalm 23. If "green pastures" meant belly-deep alfalfa, as people often picture, it would signal that God is plopping you down in a place where you would never need anything more for the rest of your life. The "green pastures" of reality, however, mean that the sheep have what they need for that day, and then they have to trust the shepherd to lead them further down the paths for more grass later. "In the desert, you learn the shepherd will get you what you need for right now," Vander Laan says. "Ten minutes from now, you trust the shepherd."[10]

Psalm 23 portrays a shepherd—and a God—who is not only loving but also assertive. The final verse says that the shepherd's love will "follow" him—sometimes translated "pursue" him—all the days of his life. William P. Brown writes, "God's benevolence takes on an aggressive quality. The metaphor of pursuit, as applied to God, effectively displaces the role that the enemies once had. The speaker joyously declares being the target not of enemies but of God's love, from which there is no escape. In dogged pursuit, God's benevolence will track down to secure and bless the speaker."[11]

The good shepherd carefully prepares for ways to make his sheep thrive. He chooses the right paths. He brings his rod and staff, which comfort the sheep and also rescue, discipline, and protect them from predators. He anoints their heads with oil in order to keep flies and dangerous parasites away. He prepares a "table," or as Keller interprets it, "high tableland," long ahead of when the sheep will arrive there, by spreading salt and minerals, preparing bedding grounds, making sure vegetation is adequate, and eradicating poisonous plants, so that when his sheep arrive, they will thrive.[12] The sheep are not aware of all this preparation, and they certainly couldn't do it themselves. They enjoy the love and provision of the shepherd. Though they are fearful and vulnerable by nature, and the world can feel like a frightening place, they fully trust the shepherd. That's how David saw the Lord. That's why this psalm is so beloved.

Psalm 23 is only six verses long, and this book of the Bible in which it appears offers 149 other psalms that are rich in praise, reflection, grief, questioning, joy, celebration, history, theology, prophecy, and inspiration. Many Bible readers are content to experience the psalms mostly in the piecemeal ways they are filtered through modern worship songs or sermons or references in popular culture. Many psalms never become as well known as Psalm 23 or a handful of others. They're never set to music or printed on posters or included in a pastor's message. Even people who think they know the psalms often really have only snacked on them. That is unfortunate, because they are far more than a feel-good verse here or there. They are a feast.

Notes

1. Lori Anne Ferrell, *The Bible and the People* (New Haven, CT: Yale University Press, 2008), 114.

2. Gerald H. Wilson, *Psalms Volume 1*, The NIV Application Commentary (Grand Rapids: Zondervan, 2002), 13.

3. Wilson, 14.

4. Wilson, 24.

5. Wilson, 31.

6. Henry Ward Beecher, *Life Thoughts* (Boston: Phillips, Sampson, 1858), 8-10, quoted in C. Hassell Bullock, *Encountering the Book of Psalms: A Literary and Theological Introduction* (Grand Rapids: Baker Academic, 2001), 171.

7. W. Phillip Keller, *A Shepherd Looks at Psalm 23* (Grand Rapids: Zondervan, 2007), 42.

8. Keller, 44.

9. Ray Vander Laan, "Understanding Green Pastures/ Shepherd Lesson/ Psalm 23," You-Tube video, 4:40, posted by "Life Lessons," May 8, 2017, https://www.youtube.com/watch?v=2x8MwiTs0hM.

10. Vander Laan.

11. William P. Brown, *Psalms* (Nashville: Abingdon Press, 2010), 35.

12. Keller, *Shepherd*, 125.

Digging Deeper

1. The psalms have been influential for centuries in Jewish and Christian congregations around the world. They were sung in the temple that Solomon built, and they continue to be sung in churches today. David sang them, and so did Jesus, Paul, Augustine, Luther, Calvin, and millions of others. What is it about the psalms that has made them so universally beloved? When you read or sing them today, do you ever get a sense of this rich history, as your voice blends with those voices from the past who have also lifted these words to God?

2. As you read the psalms of lament, such as Psalms 31, 44, and 88, how do you respond to the depth of anger and sadness these psalmists display in their outcry to God? Why are these psalms often not as well known as the more positive, celebratory psalms? Some may think the tone and content of these psalms sound disrespectful to God. How would you respond to that?

3. One significant theme in Psalm 23 is the sheep's total dependence on the shepherd. Is it hard for many people to come to terms with the idea that we are totally dependent on God? In what ways do we try to pretend otherwise? Does total dependence on God mean passivity? If not, how should it be lived out?

Go to https://www.thefoundrypublishing.com/8OT/LeaderGuide for a free downloadable leader's guide that includes more questions for reflection as well as activities for use in a small group setting.

8

Moses—"Who Am I . . . ?"

⁹ *"And now the cry of the Israelites has reached me, and I have seen the way the Egyptians are oppressing them.* ¹⁰ *So now, go. I am sending you to Pharaoh to bring my people the Israelites out of Egypt."*

¹¹ *But Moses said to God, "Who am I that I should go to Pharaoh and bring the Israelites out of Egypt?"*

¹² *And God said, "I will be with you."*

—*Exodus 3:9-12*

¹³ *Moses answered the people, "Do not be afraid. Stand firm and you will see the deliverance the* LORD *will bring you today. The Egyptians you see today you will never see again.* ¹⁴ *The* LORD *will fight for you; you need only to be still."*

—*Exodus 14:13-14*

¹ *And God spoke all these words:*

² *"I am the* LORD *your God, who brought you out of Egypt, out of the land of slavery.*

³ *"You shall have no other gods before me.*

⁴ *"You shall not make for yourself an image in the form of anything in heaven above or on the earth beneath or in the waters below.* ⁵ *You shall not bow down to them or worship them; for I, the* LORD *your God, am a jealous God, punishing the children for the sin of the parents to the third and fourth generation of those who hate me,* ⁶ *but showing love to a thousand generations of those who love me and keep my commandments.*

⁷ *"You shall not misuse the name of the* LORD *your God, for the* LORD *will not hold anyone guiltless who misuses his name.*

⁸ *"Remember the Sabbath day by keeping it holy.* ⁹ *Six days you shall labor and do all your work,* ¹⁰ *but the seventh day is a Sabbath to the* LORD *your God. On it you shall not do any work, neither you, nor your son or daughter, nor your male or female servant, nor your animals, nor any foreigner residing in your towns.* ¹¹ *For in six days the* LORD *made the heavens and the earth, the sea, and all that is in them, but he rested on the seventh day. Therefore the* LORD *blessed the Sabbath day and made it holy.*

¹² *"Honor your father and your mother, so that you may live long in the land the* LORD *your God is giving you.*

¹³ *"You shall not murder.*

¹⁴ *"You shall not commit adultery.*

¹⁵ *"You shall not steal.*

¹⁶ *"You shall not give false testimony against your neighbor.*

¹⁷ *"You shall not covet your neighbor's house. You shall not covet your neighbor's wife, or his male or female servant, his ox or donkey, or anything that belongs to your neighbor."*

—*Exodus 20:1-17*

WHO IS THE REAL MOSES? When you hear his name, what image first comes to mind? I asked that question on social media. The responses were wide ranging: baby Moses in a basket on the Nile; a white-bearded, robed man holding a staff; a burning bush; Moses holding the tablets of the Ten Commandments; Moses sitting as Aaron and Hur hold up his arms; Moses parting the Red Sea; Moses striking the rock; Moses smashing the tablets; Moses gazing up at the smoking Mount Sinai.

One image mentioned more than any other was Charlton Heston. That actor played Moses in the classic 1956 film *The Ten Commandments*, directed by Cecil B. DeMille. Rather than answer my question in words, some simply posted a photo or video of Heston, such as an image of the actor sporting a beard, arms spread wide, standing before the raging Red Sea as he parts it with the staff he holds in his right hand.

I have to admit that even though I had never seen the entire *Ten Commandments* movie before writing this chapter, my own image of Moses also veered toward Charlton Heston, based on all the movie excerpts and photos I have seen of him over the years. Heston's portrayal has sunk deep into the popular imagination, and he does capture certain heroic qualities of Moses, but I think there are other characteristics that he doesn't quite bring to life. His Moses is larger than life, and the film is respectful of Scripture, but for me, Heston's Moses is sometimes *too* one-dimensionally the superhero, in a stiff 1950s manner. The Moses I read about in Scripture is much more complex.

One thing that makes the Moses story irresistible—the reason so many moviemakers keep coming back to him, and painters, sculptors, novelists, poets, and songwriters have never tired of portraying him—is that he is *both* the bearded hero who parts the waters *and* he is the humble shepherd whose years of monotonous toil are shattered by the voice of God in a bush that burns but is not consumed.

The commandments that Moses brought down from Mount Sinai have been civilization changing for three thousand years. Moses's courageous confrontation with Pharaoh ultimately freed a people who had been enslaved for more than four hundred years. The horrific plagues that were necessary to overcome Pharaoh's hardened heart as Moses persistently demanded the release of God's people displayed to the whole world for all time that God would not abandon his people. The years-long, eventful, and sometimes torturous journey from Egypt to the edge of the promised land solidified that people, helped them finally break free of their slave mentality, and ultimately gave the next generation the courage to enter the land God had prepared for them.

But that same history-changing Moses also questioned God—repeatedly, and with one excuse after another—about whether he was the right one to lead the people. He also killed a man and had to flee to the desert alone, afraid of punishment by Pharaoh. He showed up in Midian friendless and without any known prospects for the future. He had a temper that got him in trouble. His trust in God faltered a time or two. He was a hero, but not a superhero. He was a fully human person who trusted God. His great deeds make him worthy of our attention, but so do the small, human moments of insecurity, doubt, faith, and love. My own faith is strengthened just as much by studying the insecure or angry or personally courageous Moses as it is admiring the leader holding up the staff or the tablets in front of the crowds.

Some scenes from Moses's life are compelling because they show a combination of the exalted leader and the self-doubting little guy. Those are the scenes that make me love Moses the most, and I want to consider two of them, looking at how Exodus presents them as well as how some filmmakers over the last sixty years have interpreted them.

Speaking to the Voice in the Fire

The story of Moses seems vast, filled with miracles, journeys, plagues, and countless other details, but it is actually presented in succinct, economical prose in the Bible. Decades of action can take place in one chapter. One scene from Moses's life that writers, painters, and filmmakers have retold countless times in a variety of creative ways is when Moses encounters God in the burning bush.

Moses is already eighty years old by the time he sees the bush that burns but is not consumed, and many important moments of his life have already taken place. Those dramatic events go all the way back to his birth. He survived Pharaoh's attempt to kill him and all the other male Hebrew newborns in order to curb the population of Hebrew slaves, who had become so numerous that the Egyptian leaders feared them. Moses's mother hid him for three months but then prepared a basket for him so that he could float down the river and be rescued. Moses's sister watched as the basket reached Pharaoh's daughter, who, accompanied by her attendants, came to bathe in the Nile. This daughter of Pharaoh felt sorry for the baby. Moses's sister arranged for Moses's own mother to be hired to nurse him, and then Pharaoh's daughter named him Moses and raised him as her own.

Moses grew up in Pharaoh's household, but one day he saw an Egyptian beating a Hebrew. Moses killed him and hid the body in the sand. Pharaoh found out and wanted to kill Moses, so Moses fled to Midian alone. He came to the rescue of some sisters at a well. He met their father, and before long, he married one of the girls, Zipporah, and they had a son. Moses worked tending the flocks of his father-in-law Jethro.

All of that action, the subject of countless paintings and films and Sunday school lessons and children's books, takes years to unfold, but it fills only two chapters and one verse in Exodus.

One detail from those forty-eight verses I have not mentioned is that during those long years of Moses's time in Midian, the pharaoh who wanted to kill him died, and God heard the groaning of his Hebrew people and "remembered his covenant with Abraham, with Isaac and with Jacob. So God looked on the Israelites and was concerned about them" (Exodus 2:24-25).

Moses was minding his own business, watching the flocks and working to take care of his wife and child, when he came across a fire in that harsh landscape that would change not only his own life but also the history of the world. Here is where the Bible's scarcity of details makes me wish I could fill some in. What was Moses thinking about in the hours leading up to this fateful encounter? Did he have a sense of destiny, or did he expect this to be a day like any other, following flocks around until the workday was over? Was he bored? Did he believe the most momentous days of his life were already far behind him? Did he expect to ever see Egypt again? Did he think he would ever do anything in his life that anyone outside his immediate family would remember?

What about this most famous bush in history? The book of Exodus gives us only one simple verse: "There the angel of the LORD appeared to him in flames of fire from within a bush. Moses saw that though the bush was on fire it did not burn up" (3:2). Not too impressive as miracles go. No big spectacle. In fact, the bush is so low key that some filmmakers have chosen to give it a bit more of a dazzling Hollywood treatment. In the animated film *The Prince of Egypt*, the fire in the bush starts off subtle, as Moses touches the flames that do not harm his fingers.

But as God speaks from within the light, with his voice going from a whisper to a deeper, more soothing voice, and eventually to a shout, the flame also changes. When God promises that he will go with Moses, the light envelops Moses in a caressing way, but when God demands that Moses set aside his objections and *go*, the light bursts forward, knocking Moses down. As God reveals his plans for Moses, the light swirls up toward the sky, encompassing everything before it finally disappears, leaving Moses alone in the daylight to consider what he has experienced.[1]

In the 2014 Moses film, *Exodus: Gods and Kings*, Moses is skeptical of faith and religion in the scenes leading up to the burning bush. Not long before he sees the bush, Moses plays outside with his son Gershom, who looks toward Mount Sinai and asks his father whether he has ever been to the top of it. Moses says no and asks Gershom whether he would like to. The boy answers that his mother says God does not allow it. Moses skeptically asks, "Our God stops us from climbing mountains?" Not *every* mountain, the boy answers. "Just that one. It's God's mountain." Zipporah later scolds Moses for showing his skepticism in front of the boy, but the bush scene will change Moses's mind.[2]

Moses soon gets his chance to climb that mountain when he has to chase some stray animals in a dark storm. A landslide knocks him down and buries him in mud. When he regains consciousness from this accident, only his face shows through the mud. That's when he sees the burning bush. It is the smallest and simplest of the burning bushes of any of the major film versions of the story. The voice comes not from the bush itself, but from God's messenger, in the form of a boy named Malak. He delivers the message that he needs a general—to fight. He says that Moses should go and see what is happening to his people. "Who are you?" asks Moses. "I Am," says the boy, and then he disappears. As he does so, the mud covers Moses's face.[3]

Was the encounter at the bush real or imagined? The next scene shows Moses shivering in bed, his leg broken, as his wife tells him he was hit on the head and that anything he saw, or thinks he saw, after that was only an effect of that injury. But Moses, previously skeptical of the supernatural, now is a changed man. He believes.

Cecil B. DeMille's *The Ten Commandments* also veers from Scripture somewhat in how Moses approaches God at the bush. In the film, as Moses kneels before the orange glow of the bush, he asks, "Lord, why do you not hear the cries of their children in the bondage of Egypt?"[4]

In that telling, Moses is boldly taking the initiative in confronting God about the plight of the Hebrew people. But Exodus presents it much differently. In Exodus 3, when God speaks of being the God of Abraham, Isaac, and Jacob, Moses hides his face out of fear of looking at God. He says nothing. It is God who takes the first step of telling Moses his intention to answer the cry of the Israelites and to lead them to the promised land. God breaks into this shepherd's familiar routine and announces that Moses is the leader he has chosen. Moses does not approach God. God approaches Moses.

God does not give a direct answer to Moses's question, "Who am I that I should go to Pharaoh and bring the Israelites out of Egypt?" (3:11). A direct response would address Moses's qualifications or identity. Instead, God answers, "I will be with you" (v. 12).

My faith soars when I read that. God doesn't need Moses or anyone else to prove their heroic stature or worth to carry out his will. He needs those he calls only to trust him enough to know that he will be with them.

In *The Ten Commandments*, the Charlton Heston Moses does articulate some of the objections that Moses raises in Exodus, but the tone the film uses with those objections is more akin to Moses simply asking for clarification and guidance. Moses says, "Who am I, Lord, that you should send me? How can I lead these people out of bondage? What words can I speak that they will heed?" God responds, "I will teach thee what thou wilt say."[5]

That exchange sounds like an up-and-coming leader asking the boss how to handle a delicate situation, but I think Moses's crisis of self-doubt is deeper in Exodus. He needs not only a script to speak but, more importantly, the knowledge that he must rely, not on himself and his own skills, but on God.

Of the three films I have mentioned, *The Prince of Egypt* is most faithful to the tone and message of the burning-bush scene. It captures Moses's sense of awe in the presence of God, represented by all that swirling light.

Moses's objections tumble out of him all at once when God calls him to confront Pharaoh. Moses concludes by saying, "You've chosen the wrong messenger. How can I even speak to these people?" At that instant, the light from the bush bursts forth in brilliant anger, knocking Moses down, and the booming voice of God, tinged with anger, shouts, "Who made man's mouth? Who made the deaf, the mute, the seeing, or the blind? Did not I? Now go!" The scene ends with a more reassuring voice from God, promising Moses he will be with him, empowering him to do wonders among the Egyptians.[6]

The burning-bush scene in *Exodus: Gods and Kings*, while powerful in its own way, leaves out Moses's objections altogether. It is an unfortunate omission because it downplays some important truths about how God works in the lives of believers even now.

Moses's objections—and his ultimate decision to set them aside and obey God in spite of all the difficulties he will face as a result—reveal a particular kind of faith. It is different from the faith that David showed when he volunteered to fight the giant that everyone else was too afraid to confront. David jumped into that fight confidently, even eagerly, relying on his past successes with fighting lions and bears and his knowledge that God would be with him. Moses's faith is also different from the total, unquestioning trust in God that Abraham showed when he willingly took Isaac up the mountain to sacrifice him.

The kinds of doubts Moses raises can be found in certain other biblical narratives that describe God's call. Jeremiah and Isaiah both speak of their unworthiness for the call, for example. But Moses's objections, which are spelled out so specifically, with God responding to them one at a time, are deep, and despite all of God's reassurances, Moses appears to be on the verge of saying no to God.

From a purely human perspective, Moses's objections to his call make sense. He asks, Who am I to do this? He has a point. On his own, he has no special authority or abilities. He is not even living in Egypt anymore. He asks, What if they don't believe that God has really called me? That's a sensible question. He has no witnesses to this burning-bush encounter. Why *should* anyone believe him? Moses also objects that he is not eloquent. He is slow of speech and tongue. If God is choosing a spokesperson, shouldn't he choose someone who speaks well?

God responds to each of these objections. He will be with Moses, he will provide him with the staff that will allow Moses to perform signs and wonders, and he will provide Aaron to help him with the speaking duties. In the midst of God's response to Moses about his slowness of tongue, Moses's confidence appears to collapse, in spite of all God's promises. He says, "Pardon your servant, Lord. Please send someone else" (Exodus 4:13).

God has been patient, but now he has had enough. "Then the LORD's anger burned against Moses," according to Exodus 4:14. However, the Lord does not do what Moses asks and send someone else. He sends Moses. God knows exactly what he is doing. He knows the endless troubles Moses will face, but he also knows this is the man who will see this assignment through and get the Israelites freed and off to the promised land. This time God doesn't wait for another objection, nor is Moses recorded as actually saying yes. The conversation ends, and Moses begins his work.

God could have gotten rid of Pharaoh without Moses. He could have simply struck Pharaoh dead and set the Israelites free himself. He didn't need the hardening of Pharaoh's heart or the ten plagues—all those frogs and lice and boils and locusts and the deaths of the firstborn of Egypt— that were still to come. But God was doing something more than just getting Pharaoh out of the way or freeing the people from Pharaoh's grip. God was dramatically establishing for the Israelites that he is their God and they are his people—and he was doing so before the entire world for all time. He tells them through Moses, "I will take you as my own people, and I will be your God. Then you will know that I am the LORD your God, who brought you out from under the yoke of the Egyptians. And I will bring you to the land I swore with uplifted hand to give to Abraham, to Isaac and to Jacob. I will give it to you as a possession. I am the LORD" (6:7-8).

The brilliance of the book of Exodus is that it establishes Moses as a historic national leader while portraying him as an overwhelmed, humble follower of God. Another of the episodes of his life that combines this epic grandeur with an intimate portrayal of faith is in Moses's parting of the Red Sea.

The Lord Will Fight for You; You Need Only to Be Still

Moses stands, arms raised, staff in hand, and lying in front of him is a strip of land with two walls of water rising into the air on either side.

How many times have you seen that image? Few details of Moses's life have been painted, filmed, told, or written about as often as his parting of the Red Sea. People know that image even if they have never heard the whole story of the exodus or even if they can't quite remember why that body of water is splitting open. It almost makes him look as if he has superpowers. Like some Marvel Comics hero, he is able to carve a dry strip of land right through a sea, and he does it simply by holding up his magic staff!

It is, of course, the Lord's power, not Moses's, that pushes back the waters. And when Moses stretches out his hand over the water at the Lord's command, he isn't doing it to impress anyone or display superhuman abilities. He would rather not be in the tight spot that he's in. He is leading a complaining, frightened people over whom he is about to lose control. He has a powerful army bearing down on him. He is trying to survive. The outcome will solidify his authority as leader over those people. It will end his Pharaoh problem—which he thought was already behind him—for good. And it will provide lessons in faith that can still change our own relationship to God today.

After all that Moses and the Hebrew people had been through—centuries of slavery, one plague after another to persuade the stubborn pharaoh to release them, the complete uprooting of their lives as they prepared to quickly move to a new land—it would be hard to blame them if they thought they were due for some smooth sailing. Maybe they could make a dash across the desert and get settled into the promised land in no time.

Little did they know the many obstacles and years that still faced them. Little could they have imagined that one of the early challenges would come from their old nemesis, Pharaoh. Hadn't he gotten sick of all the trouble they brought on him by now? In the end, hadn't he not simply *allowed* them to leave but also *ordered* them to do so?

Pharaoh just couldn't quit. He had lost a valuable slave labor force and now regretted it. He sent his soldiers to recapture them, armed with weaponry and chariots that far outmatched anything the ex-slaves had at their disposal. Why did Moses order the people to camp beside the Red Sea anyhow, where Pharaoh's army could trap them?

Moses camped the people there because God ordered him to. Pharaoh had one agenda, and God had another. God was setting up this perilous situation so that "the Egyptians will know that I am the LORD"

(Exodus 14:4). God had every intention of saving the Israelites and destroying Pharaoh's army. But the people didn't know the details of his plans. So when they saw this army rushing toward them, they panicked. "They were terrified and cried out to the LORD," Exodus 14:10 says. Who could blame them? They faced almost certain defeat.

However, this was the same group of people who had seen God act on their behalf many times before. They had seen the miracles of the plagues. They had seen God accomplish their own freedom after hundreds of years of bondage. Each day they saw God's presence right in front of them in a pillar of cloud that guided them on their journey, and each night they saw him in a pillar of fire. Miracles! Maybe they could trust him to do one more and defeat Pharaoh's army.

Trust was not on their minds. Instead, in their fear, they resorted to blame and to sarcasm. They complain to Moses, "Was it because there were no graves in Egypt that you brought us to the desert to die? What have you done to us by bringing us out of Egypt? Didn't we say to you in Egypt, 'Leave us alone; let us serve the Egyptians'? It would have been better for us to serve the Egyptians than to die in the desert!" (vv. 11-12).

Nowhere in the entire story of the exodus do I love Moses more than I do when I read his response to this nasty criticism. As a Christian who believes that these Old Testament stories reveal how God relates to his followers even today, I find Moses's words even more meaningful and impressive than the sea-parting miracle itself. He could have lashed out at them with the same bitter sarcasm with which they had assaulted him. He could have scolded them for being ungrateful, untruthful (had they really wanted to stay and serve the Egyptians?), and insubordinate.

Instead, he speaks these wise and reassuring words: "Do not be afraid. Stand firm and you will see the deliverance the LORD will bring you today. The Egyptians you see today you will never see again. The LORD will fight for you; you need only to be still" (vv. 13-14). Moses is acknowledging that this crisis is far beyond their ability to resolve it in their own strength. Without God's intervention, their defeat is assured. Their one hope is to trust in the Lord's deliverance. He will fight for them. So even though their instincts call for them to be terrified, and even though they may be tempted to lash out or run around frantically, what they really need to do is to be still and trust the God who has brought them through so much already. If they *really* believe he is fighting for them, then they need only to watch in gratitude to see how he will do it. They can't conceive of his solution on their own, nor can they bring it about. He will fight for them.

Those words have guided me in many crises of my own life and faith. Although there are certainly times when God calls for *action* from his followers, some situations are so enormous and complex that I sense him calling for me only to trust him and let him fight for me. I feel him encouraging me to set aside my panic and see how he will bring about a resolution that is beyond anything I could even know to ask for. It isn't easy to take my hands off a situation and calm the beating drums of my own terror as I turn it over to God. But I have known him to replace my panic with the peace that comes from the Holy Spirit as I await his intervention.

The countless videos, cartoons, children's books, movies, stained-glass windows, coloring books, and other depictions of this scene usually don't emphasize those particular words of Moses. The visual elements of the walls of water, the Israelites hurrying through the gap, and Pharaoh's chariots riding into that trap only to be inundated when the waters crash back down on them are simply too dramatic for artists to resist.

In *The Ten Commandments*, whose 1950s-era special effects often look amateurish to today's audiences, Moses's parting of the Red Sea is one of the most realistic and impressive scenes in the film. *The Prince of Egypt* film depicts the sea parting as a sudden miracle. Moses steps out into the water and hears the voice of the Lord say, "With this staff, you shall do my wonders." Moses stabs his staff into the water, and the water sprays up dramatically, forming walls higher than the eye can see.[7] *Exodus: Gods and Kings* goes for a more realistic approach, with the waters moving overnight, the way Scripture says it happened. But in this film, unlike in the book of Exodus, Moses goes to sleep that night believing he has failed. He is as surprised as anyone when the waters gradually recede enough to allow the people through. This miracle is not one of sudden walls of water allowing a clear, dry path down the middle. The people have to walk through water that is waist high at points. Moses urges the people to cross, assuring them that "God is with us." The further they go, the more the water recedes. The walls of water do not appear until they crash like gigantic waves to complete the violent, dramatic annihilation of Pharaoh's army.[8]

In Exodus 14, the miracle accomplishes what God intended it to: "And when the Israelites saw the mighty hand of the LORD displayed against the Egyptians, the people feared the LORD and put their trust in him and in Moses his servant" (v. 31). Fear, sarcasm, and complaints were set aside, but as usual, the people's increased confidence in God and Moses was temporary. There was still a long, hard journey ahead.

The Ten Commandments

As renowned as those stories are, they have not had as big an impact on the world as one other action of God in which Moses played an important role. In the popular imagination, if Moses is not holding his staff in his upraised hands, then he is probably holding the stone tablets on which God inscribed the Ten Commandments. You can probably picture those tablets right now, even if you might feel challenged to remember all ten of the commandments carved into them.

The cultural impact of the Ten Commandments has been enormous. Kevin DeYoung, author of a recent book on them, writes, "It's no exaggeration to say that these Ten Words handed down at Mount Sinai have been the most influential law code ever given."[9] He points out that Moses and the Ten Commandments are found on at least three architectural features of the United States Supreme Court building alone.

For all their historical importance, the Ten Commandments are also almost always enveloped in controversy, especially in the United States. We live in a time in which the controversies over the public displays of the Ten Commandments may be even more prominent than the commandments themselves. Those displays have been the source of political battles for decades, and such a battle is almost always happening somewhere in the nation.

In 2018, Alabama voted an amendment to the state constitution "authorizing the display of the Ten Commandments on state property and property owned or administrated by a public school or public body; and prohibiting the expenditure of public funds in defense of the constitutionality of this amendment."[10] Despite that language, groups such as the American Civil Liberties Union immediately challenged the constitutionality of the amendment.

In 2015, the Oklahoma Supreme Court ruled that a Ten Commandments monument on statehouse grounds was unconstitutional. The year before that, a judge ruled that a three-thousand-pound Ten Commandments monument on the front lawn of the city hall in Bloomfield, New Mexico, would have to be removed. In 2005, the United States Supreme Court ruled (five to four) that a Ten Commandments monument on the state capitol in Austin, Texas, could remain because it had a historical rather than a purely religious purpose. One year earlier, public schools and courthouses in Kentucky were barred from displaying copies of the Ten Commandments in those buildings because judges ruled that people who saw them might consider them a government endorsement of religion.[11] I could give many other examples of fights like these across the country.

With all of that resistance to the display of these words, why do people find it so important to continue this fight? The American Center for Law and Justice (ACLJ), a conservative Christian advocacy group, explained its own motivation in support of the displays: "There is a growing desire to display the Ten Commandments in all public venues because they traditionally have represented a moral floor for acceptable behavior and served as an antecedent to obedience to law."[12] The ACLJ believes a focus on the Ten Commandments in schools will encourage good citizenship and character education.

Those who advocate for the public displays of the commandments often emphasize their historical importance and their moral grounding. Those who oppose the displays argue that they amount to a government endorsement of a particular religion. The specifics of how the individual commandments would be translated into legislation are usually not central to the debate. It is certainly clear to see how commandments such as "Do not murder" or "Do not steal" could be translated into legislation, but few people are advocating state or federal laws against making graven images or coveting a neighbor's possessions. Few people are calling for the imprisonment of those who take the Lord's name in vain. For many advocates, the Ten Commandments monuments are symbolic of moral law in general, beyond just the actual words carved into them.

But what *are* those words? Where did they come from, and what is their purpose? Why are these ten commandments more important than all the hundreds of other laws in the Bible? For all the passion the Ten Commandments arouse in the political arena, much of what people think they know about them is wrong. Kevin DeYoung points to a recent survey that showed that only 14 percent of Americans could even name the Ten Commandments. That is fewer than the number who knew the seven ingredients in the Big Mac, the names of the six Brady Bunch children, or the names of the Three Stooges.[13]

Many scholars believe the phrase "ten commandments" would be more accurately translated "ten words" or "ten statements." The Ten Commandments do not represent all the laws given to the Israelites. Hundreds more come later—some calculate more than six hundred. But the Ten Words form the basis for those laws. As Leon R. Kass explains it, the Decalogue, as the Ten Commandments are sometimes called, "functions rather as a prologue or preamble to the constituting law. Like the preamble to the Constitution of the United States, it enunciates the general principles on which the new covenant will be founded, principles that in this case touch upon—and connect—the relation both between man and God and between man and man."[14]

Given the idea that the Ten Commandments are intended to capture those general principles that form the foundation for the rest of the law, the particular commandments that God chose to present to his people on that dramatic day at Mount Sinai may look strange to modern readers. If people today had never seen the Ten Commandments and were asked to form a committee to come up with their own version of the top commandments God would want, they would likely come up with a very different list. Prohibitions against lying and murder and theft might be in there, but others might not make it. Honoring your father and mother sounds like a good idea, for example, but does it really deserve a place in the top ten? And what's this about not making "an image in the form of anything in heaven above or on the earth beneath or in the waters below" (Exodus 20:4)? Is doing that really so common that it needs its own commandment? And misusing the Lord's name, or using the Lord's name in vain, as we have traditionally heard it, is certainly disrespectful, but does God really consider it *that* big of an offense?

The first commandment is, "You shall have no other gods before me" (v. 3). "Before me" is sometimes translated "besides me." The phrase "before me" also might carry the sense of flaunting a god before God's face. Our relationship with God must be exclusive, the way a marriage is exclusive between two people. You can't serve God *and* other gods, as the Israelites were (and many of us are) prone to do. You have to choose.

That leads logically and directly to the second commandment: "You shall not make for yourself an image in the form of anything in heaven above or on the earth beneath or in the waters below" (v. 4). These days most of us don't have little carved gods to worship, but that doesn't mean we aren't breaking this commandment. Idolatry has to do with what we put our trust in. What do we think saves us? Where do we find our ultimate identity and meaning? To what do we devote our lives?

Our idols may even have a physical form. Your idol may be a video game console or a sports jersey or a television screen. It's not that God demands that we care about nothing but him, but he wants to be our highest commitment. We worship only him and not those other things, even inadvertently. In fact, when we do worship those idols, it usually *is* inadvertent. We wouldn't admit that video games or politics or sports have pushed aside our commitment to God, but we let it happen anyway.

Dennis Prager, in his commentary on Exodus, writes that *"when anything is made an end in itself, rather than as a means to God and goodness . . . it is a false god."*[15] What do you live for? What is the *real* focus of your life, at its core? Who or what do you *really* worship? Almost none of us would worship a scary-looking piece of carved wood. Instead, we're more prone to take something *good* in our lives and elevate it to a place that only God should fill. That's what makes this kind of idolatry so alluring and therefore so dangerous.

What about the commandment that you should not take the Lord's name in vain? As a kid, I thought it meant not cussing, especially if the cuss word or phrase included "God" in it. A no-no for sure, but one of the Ten Commandments? Kevin DeYoung writes that this third commandment prohibits us from "taking the name of God (or *taking up* the name or *bearing* the name, as the phrase could be translated) in a manner that is wicked, worthless, or for wrongful purposes."[16] One way we can break this commandment is by falsely ascribing our own ideas, prejudices, or plans to God in order to claim more authority for them. Another way to break it is to use his name frivolously, such as when we say a flippant prayer without really keeping in mind to whom we are praying. Cursing with God's name or using his name mockingly in other ways also violates the commandment. We may live in an irreverent age that doesn't take God's name very seriously, but God does. Taking God's name in vain goes beyond how we might use a word or phrase that mentions him. It also encompasses how we live. Claiming an identity as a Christian but then living in un-Christlike ways is a form of using God's name in vain.

Remembering the Sabbath by keeping it holy is another concept that is important to God even though it can be bewildering to the modern mindset. Leon R. Kass writes, "Of all the statements in the Decalogue, the one regarding the Sabbath is the most far-reaching and the most significant. It addresses the profound matters of time and its reckoning, work and rest, and man's relation to God, the world, and his fellow men."[17] This commandment is the longest and most detailed of all of them. Kass points out that the word "sabbath" comes from a root word that means "to cease" or "to rest." Think of what that must have meant to the Israelite ex-slaves hearing this commandment for the first time. They had never been allowed to determine when, if ever, they could take a day to rest, and now they were being commanded to do so.

The commandment specifically mentions the Lord's creation of "the heavens and the earth, the sea, and all that is in them" in six days. On the seventh day he rested (Exodus 20:11). So the Sabbath honors and celebrates that loving and awesome cycle of creation and rest. The world, even in its fallen state, is not only about toil and productivity. The people who first heard this commandment had been slaves, valued only for the work they could produce, but they no longer had to define themselves that way. They could follow the rhythm of God's creation. It would be not only a day of ceasing from work but also a Sabbath unto the Lord, in which they would worship and honor him. Today, we mark the Sabbath in various ways, but those principles still hold.

Most of the commandments tell us what *not* to do—do not steal, do not murder, do not lie, do not commit adultery—but along with the Sabbath commandment, the other one that tells us to *do* something is the one that commands that we honor our father and mother. Unlike any other commandment, this one identifies a specific reward for this behavior. You are to honor your parents "so that you may live long in the land the LORD your God is giving you" (v. 12). Prager argues that the promise is not for the individual but for the whole community and that this commandment, with its emphasis on the importance of family, helps to preserve and extend that community. He writes, "The commandment promises the nation collectively that if its members honor their parents, the family will be preserved, its religious traditions and beliefs will be preserved, and the civilization will therefore long endure. The breakdown of the family is a guarantor of the breakdown of a civilization."[18]

How does this commandment account for parents who are abusive or irresponsible? Kass points out that the command is not to "admire" or "love" or even "obey" the parents. It is to honor them. This commandment follows the one about the Sabbath, which is a celebration of the cycle of God's creation of the world, for which we are to be grateful. Honoring one's parents celebrates, in a sense, our own creation, since our parents helped make it come about. We are to honor their part in that creation, and honor the very concept of the God-created roles of father and mother.[19]

While most of the commandments deal with actions, the final commandment, which prohibits coveting anything that belongs to our neighbor, whether it be possessions or relationships, focuses specifically on thoughts and motivations. If thoughts are going to be included in the Ten Commandments, why coveting in particular? Why not lust or greed or apathy or another attitude that is also wrong? Prager says that to covet means "to desire to the point of seeking to take something that belongs to another person." It's not just that you want a fancy car but that you want your neighbor's fancy car, and you want it so much that you are willing to plot how to get it. This commandment follows those against committing adultery, stealing, and lying, and it identifies a major motivation behind violating those prohibitions.[20]

Who Is Moses?

When God called Moses from the burning bush, one of Moses's questions to God began with the phrase, "Who am I . . . ?" The answer to that question could fill entire books. Although he has often been reduced to the heroic but rather stiff figure holding up tablets or dividing a sea, those moments are only the public side of him. He was also a man of deep faith who longed to see God and to know him. He loved his people, and he loved his God. Repeatedly, God pushed Moses beyond his own capabilities, but Moses learned to press forward with the kind of faith that still inspires and instructs us today.

Notes

1. *The Prince of Egypt*, directed by Brenda Chapman, Steve Hickner, and Simon Wells (Glendale, CA: Dreamworks Animation, 1998).

2. *Exodus: Gods and Kings*, directed by Ridley Scott (Los Angeles: Twentieth Century Fox, 2014).

3. *Exodus: Gods and Kings*.

4. *The Ten Commandments*, directed by Cecil B. DeMille (Hollywood, CA: Paramount Pictures, 1956).

5. *Ten Commandments*.

6. *Prince of Egypt*.

7. *Prince of Egypt*.

8. *Exodus: Gods and Kings*.

9. Kevin DeYoung, *The Ten Commandments: What They Mean, Why They Matter, and Why We Should Obey Them* (Wheaton, IL: Crossway, 2018), 16.

10. Scott Slayton, "Alabama Voters Approve Public Displays of the Ten Commandments," November 8, 2018, Christianheadlines.com, https://www.christianheadlines.com/contributors /scott-slayton/alabama-voters-approve-public-displays-of-the-ten-commandments.html (November 29, 2018).

11. Erica Getto and Kavish Harjai, "8 Times That a 10 Commandments Monument Had Its Day in Court," July 8, 2015, MSNBC.com, http://www.msnbc.com/msnbc/8-times-10 -commandments-monument-had-its-day-court (November 29, 2018).

12. "Ten Commandments Displays in Public Places," June 16, 2011, American Center for Law and Justice, https://aclj.org/10-commandments/ten-commandments-displays-in-public -places (November 29, 2018).

13. DeYoung, *Ten Commandments*, 16.

14. Leon R. Kass, "The Ten Commandments: Why the Decalogue Matters," June 3, 2013, American Enterprise Institute, https://www.aei.org/articles/the-ten-commandments-why-the -decalogue-matters/ (November 30, 2018).

15. Dennis Prager, *Exodus: God, Slavery, and Freedom*, The Rational Bible, ed. Joseph Telushkin, The Alperson Edition (Washington, DC: Regnery Faith, 2018), 228.

16. DeYoung, *Ten Commandments*, 53.

17. Kass, "Ten Commandments."

18. Prager, *Exodus*, 258.

19. Kass, "Ten Commandments."

20. Prager, *Exodus*, 272-73.

Digging Deeper

1. Which aspect of Moses do you find yourself most drawn to, the historical national leader who frees his people, or the overwhelmed, humble follower of God who has some insecurities and isn't quite sure he is up to the task? Why does the Bible show both?

2. Moses's story shows that some situations call for bold and courageous action, such as when he confronts Pharaoh. Other situations, however, require him to be still and trust God, such as when Pharaoh's army is bearing down on Moses's people by the Red Sea. Review the words of Exodus 14:13-14. Can you think of a dilemma you confronted that was so beyond any solution you could imagine that all you could do was trust God to rescue you? What was the outcome? How can you tell the difference between situations that call for action and situations that call for stillness and trust?

3. This chapter quotes a commentator who declares that the Ten Commandments are the most influential law code ever given. But if people today were to start from scratch and speculate on which ten laws might be the most important ones to God, they might come up with a very different list. "Do not murder" and "Do not steal" seem obvious, but others, such as a prohibition on graven images, may seem strange to modern readers. In what ways does this chapter show that *all* the Ten Commandments are crucial and still relevant today?

Go to https://www.thefoundrypublishing.com/8OT/LeaderGuide for a free downloadable leader's guide that includes more questions for reflection as well as activities for use in a small group setting.

9

Jonah Leaving the Whale // Jan Brueghel the Elder // c. 1568–1625

Jonah—
More Than a Fish Tale

¹⁰ And the LORD *commanded the fish, and it vomited Jonah onto dry land.*

¹ Then the word of the LORD *came to Jonah a second time: ² "Go to the great city of Nineveh and proclaim to it the message I give you."*

³ Jonah obeyed the word of the LORD *and went to Nineveh. Now Nineveh was a very large city; it took three days to go through it. ⁴ Jonah began by going a day's journey into the city, proclaiming, "Forty more days and Nineveh will be overthrown." ⁵ The Ninevites believed God. A fast was proclaimed, and all of them, from the greatest to the least, put on sackcloth.*

⁶ When Jonah's warning reached the king of Nineveh, he rose from his throne, took off his royal robes, covered himself with sackcloth and sat down in the dust. ⁷ This is the proclamation he issued in Nineveh:

"By the decree of the king and his nobles:

Do not let people or animals, herds or flocks, taste anything; do not let them eat or drink. ⁸ But let people and animals be covered with sackcloth. Let everyone call urgently on God. Let them give up their evil ways and their violence. ⁹ Who knows? God may yet relent and with compassion turn from his fierce anger so that we will not perish."

¹⁰ When God saw what they did and how they turned from their evil ways, he relented and did not bring on them the destruction he had threatened.

¹ But to Jonah this seemed very wrong, and he became angry. ² He prayed to the LORD, *"Isn't this what I said,* LORD, *when I was still at home? That is what I tried to forestall by fleeing to Tarshish. I knew that you are a gracious and compassionate God, slow to anger and abounding in love, a God who relents from sending calamity. ³ Now,* LORD, *take away my life, for it is better for me to die than to live."*

⁴ But the LORD *replied, "Is it right for you to be angry?"*

—Jonah 2:10–4:4

ASK PEOPLE to complete the phrase "Noah and the _____," and almost everyone will come up with the word "ark." Ask them to complete the phrase "Jonah and the _____," and they are almost certain to answer "whale." Whether they have read the story in the Bible for themselves, or whether they could even *find* the story in the Bible, they will know about that whale. One problem with this "whale" is that the biblical story says that God "provided a huge fish" (1:17), not a whale. So Jonah's whale is the most famous whale in history, even though it isn't even a whale.

Jonah's "whale" has become internationally famous, even though the biblical story provides little information about it. In the New International Version, only three sentences deal directly with the fish. The first two are,

"Now the LORD provided a huge fish to swallow Jonah, and Jonah was in the belly of the fish three days and three nights. From inside the fish Jonah prayed to the LORD his God" (Jonah 1:17–2:1). Then Jonah's prayer is given, followed by the final sentence about the fish: "And the LORD commanded the fish, and it vomited Jonah onto dry land" (2:10). That's it. The fish swallows him, Jonah spends three days and nights inside, and the fish vomits him out.

Ever since then, painters, poets, Sunday school teachers, filmmakers, and storytellers of every kind have used their own imaginations to determine what that fish looked like and what Jonah endured inside it for three days. The narrator of the book of Jonah doesn't give any of those details.

Would this story be as popular and famous if it had no "whale" in it? I believe that God uses the Bible to speak to human beings—to give them a sense of who he is, to instruct them, to tell them his story of redemption, to inspire them. As we have seen, he uses many genres to do this—parables, prophecies, histories, biographies, laws, poetry. People are drawn to animals, and biblical stories that include animals are some of the most memorable parts of Scripture. These stories have had a huge impact on popular and artistic culture. Noah's ark, filled with all those animals, is beloved around the world. Many people have heard or read the story of Balaam's donkey. The great sea beast Leviathan is celebrated in the book of Job.

Although the "whale" gets much of the attention in popular retellings of the story of Jonah, the biblical story is magnificent for reasons that go far beyond a fish. As we'll see, the story is about many things. It's about forgiveness. It's about "a gracious and compassionate God, slow to anger and abounding in love, a God who relents from sending calamity" (Jonah 4:2). It's about God's concern not only for humanity but for all of creation. It's about how God uses strange and sometimes harsh wake-up calls to get us spiritually back on track. It illustrates the truth that if we would obey God to begin with, we would save ourselves lots of trouble. It shows that a force that looks as if it might destroy us may actually be a provision sent by God to rescue us. It's about the sovereignty of God. It's about the fact that just because we're angry doesn't mean we're right. It's about how running from God is futile. It's about God's belief in second chances, and it's about how he loves people that we can't stand.

All those lessons and more are packed into those four short chapters of the book, but audiences are focused on that "whale"! One reason the big fish has reached such heights of popularity is that it makes the story child friendly. It's like those cute animals in Noah's story, marching into the ark two-by-two. Never mind that they're doing it because the world around them is about to be demolished. The "whale" is also often depicted as cute, as he swallows Jonah, offers him a cozy place to spend a few days, and then spits him back out, unharmed, onto dry ground.

Toy makers love Jonah and the whale. Plastic whales with plastic Jonahs inside are available for purchase for vacation Bible school gifts. Want something cuddlier? How about a plush, stuffed whale with a zippered mouth, inside of which your child can hide the plush Jonah? Or maybe you would have more fun with the Jonah and the Whale Toss Game, in which you throw beanbag Jonahs into the mouth of the whale. Hit the center of the mouth and earn a hundred points! Or you can find "Jonah and the whale" finger puppets, shadow puppets, puzzles (with the Jonah piece fitting nicely inside the whale), posters, bedspreads, stickers, and jewelry.

The Jonah story is straightforward enough that it translates well as a children's story, and many children's authors have retold it successfully. *Jonah's Big Fish Adventure*, part of The Beginner's Bible series, is a board book for children aged one to four that captures in a simple and compelling way some of the key elements of the biblical story and message. Jonah is introduced as a man who "told people about God." One day God tells him to go to Nineveh because the people there are doing bad things. Jonah is scared and doesn't want to go to a place with bad people, so he runs away. He finds a ship and asks the sailors to take him with them. God sends a storm. The sailors are terrified and ask what's going on. Jonah says the storm is his fault and tells them to throw him overboard. They do, and the sea becomes calm. A giant fish comes and swallows Jonah "with one gulp." Jonah spends three days and nights in the "smelly belly" of the fish, praying to God to forgive him. God hears Jonah's prayers, and the fish spits him onto dry land. Jonah hurries to Nineveh, he speaks to the people, and they ask God for forgiveness. The story ends with "God forgave them, just as he forgave Jonah."[1] Although that version simplifies the story for its very young audience and leaves out the section about the vine and Jonah's anger at God's decision to not punish the Ninevites, it still embodies many of the themes of the biblical account.

The Hard to Swallow Tale of Jonah and the Whale, pitched to a somewhat older children's audience, does include Jonah's anger at God's compassion for the Ninevites and the lesson he teaches Jonah through the vine. The language is at a level that children can understand but that adults can also appreciate. Near the end, God confronts Jonah about his anger over the dead vine: "'O Jonah,' God said, 'if you are so troubled over the loss of a vine, think of what I feel for Nineveh—its people and animals.'" Jonah responds with silence. He looks out over the city of 120,000, which the book illustrates. Then he takes down his shelter and heads home. The book concludes, "At last he understood that the Lord's compassion had no limits. It reached from the heights of the dark, angry sea; and it stretched all the way across the world—from Tarshish in the west to Nineveh in the east."[2] Even though the biblical text doesn't include quite that much closure—Jonah's response to God's message is not given—this children's version is able to capture the message and drama of the biblical text.

One of my favorite children's versions of the Jonah story is *Jonah and the Fish*, by Dandi Mackall and Lissy Marlin. It is part of the Flipside Stories series. When you read the book in one direction, you get the tale from Jonah's point of view. When you flip the book over and read it the other direction, you get the story from the fish's perspective. Both sides of the story are told in rhyming sentences. Jonah's version focuses on his disobedience to God's command to go to Nineveh. The story follows his adventure on the ship and his time in the fish. It ends with him coming to his senses, getting spewed out onto the shore, and deciding to obey God. The fish's side of the story emphasizes his obedience in obeying God to fulfill his own part in the story. As he swims beneath the ship, he sees the man tossed overboard. The fish says, "I watched till I heard the Creator's strange plan: 'Your brave and bold deed is to swallow this man!'" The fish does so but gets worried when the man stays inside him in silence for three days. Finally he gets the command to spit the man onto the shore. "He landed—kerplop—and he tumbled a bit. Who knew my great deed would be SWALLOW AND SPIT?"[3]

Jonah and his big fish have been presented to children in many other books, videos, church lessons, games, and activities. But the impact of this story on popular culture is not limited to works for children. The story has also been popularized for adults in poems, songs, and paintings throughout the generations. The story has been captured in poetry by a diverse set of writers that include Aldous Huxley, Dietrich Bonhoeffer, Randall Jarrell, and Luci Shaw.

Perhaps not surprisingly, Herman Melville, the author of one of the most famous whale tales in history, makes many references to the Jonah story in his novel *Moby-Dick*. In chapters 7–9 of that book, Ishmael and other sailors go to the Whaleman's Chapel in the days leading up to their great voyage and hear a sermon on Jonah from Father Mapple, who was a sailor and harpooner in his youth. The congregation first sings a hymn about the story that begins,

> The ribs and terrors in the whale,
> Arched over me a dismal gloom,
> While all God's sun-lit waves rolled by,
> And lift me deepening down to doom.[4]

Father Mapple's sermon reflects the spiritual meaning of the story, but it also captures the drama of Jonah's near drowning and his being swallowed by the whale: "We feel the floods surging over us; we sound with him to the kelpy bottom of the waters; sea-weed and all the slime of the sea is about us!" Father Mapple says that Jonah's story "is a lesson to us all, because it is a story of the sin, hard-heartedness, suddenly awakened fears, the swift punishment, repentance, prayers, and finally the deliverance and joy of Jonah." One thing the preacher admires about Jonah's repentance is that Jonah first admits that his punishment is just, and he "does not weep and wail for direct deliverance." Jonah leaves his deliverance up to God, and God releases him from the whale to obey, which Jonah does.[5]

Singers and songwriters have also been captivated by Jonah and the whale. The story makes a quick appearance in the song "It Ain't Necessarily So," in George and Ira Gershwin's 1935 musical, *Porgy and Bess*. More recently, Bruce Springsteen sang about it in his song "Swallowed Up (in the Belly of the Whale)" in 2012. Because the story is so visually striking, painters and sculptors throughout the centuries have also not been able to resist offering their interpretations of some of the dramatic scenes. A Roman sarcophagus of the third century depicts Jonah being flung from the ship directly into the mouth of a fierce, sharp-toothed fish that looks more like a monster than a whale.[6] In 1621, Dutch artist Pieter Lastman showed a different part of the story in his dramatic painting *Jonah and the Whale*. His ferocious whale is shown with the naked Jonah wrapped tightly in its tongue as the fish prepares to fling Jonah up onto the land at the end of his three-day ordeal inside the creature.[7]

Jonah: Blunt, Rebellious, and on the Run

As dramatic and even as entertaining as all those artistic depictions and imaginative retellings of Jonah can be, none of them fully captures the power of the original version in the Bible itself. The story is short, but each chapter is packed with meaning. Unlike some biblical figures, there is nothing subtle about Jonah. When Abraham approaches God on behalf of Sodom and Gomorrah, for example, he speaks with careful politeness, starting his questions with phrases such as, "Now that I have been so bold as to speak to the Lord, though I am nothing but dust and ashes, what if . . ." (Genesis 18:27-28), or "May the Lord not be angry, but let me speak" (v. 30). Or when God calls Moses to confront Pharaoh and bring the Israelites out of Egypt, Moses politely pushes back: "Pardon your servant, Lord. I have never been eloquent, neither in the past nor since you have spoken to your servant" (Exodus 4:10).

Jonah is different. Throughout the story, he bluntly lets his feelings be known, not only in words but also in actions. The first act we see from Jonah, even before he speaks at all, is an act of rebellion. The book begins, "The word of the LORD came to Jonah son of Amittai: 'Go to the great city of Nineveh and preach against it, because its wickedness has come up before me.' But Jonah ran away from the LORD and headed for Tarshish" (Jonah 1:1-3). No polite requests for clarification. No negotiating. Not even any excuses. Instead, Jonah heads in exactly the opposite direction from where God had told him to go.

Jonah goes down to the port of Joppa, finds a ship headed to Tarshish, pays the fare and gets on board. *Take that, God.* What has brought about such an extreme reaction? What outrageous thing did God ask this preacher-prophet to do? Well, preach! And prophesy!

Many other Old Testament prophets could be grouchy, gloomy, doomsayers, so was the problem that Jonah dreaded the idea of speaking harsh words of judgment? No, he would have loved that. Jonah was angry for a much different reason—God wanted him to warn the Ninevites so God could save them. *Save* them? Jonah couldn't stand it. Those people *deserved* whatever horrible fate befell them. Jonah wanted no part in rescuing them. So off he went in protest.

When reading this story today, it's easy to be tough on Jonah. Was he really so mean spirited that he couldn't stand the idea that God might show mercy to the Ninevites? For most of us, "Ninevites" is just a name that carries no associations, good or bad. But for Jonah, these were truly horrible people. Nineveh was part of the Assyrian Empire, and the Assyrians were known for their grotesque cruelty to people they conquered. Biblical scholar James Bruckner details a list of atrocities that are disturbing to read. The Assyrians didn't just kill their enemies; they took pleasure in torturing them. Dismemberment was one of their favorite tactics. While the victims were still alive, the soldiers cut off noses, hands, feet. They gouged out eyes. After the victims were dead, their heads were cut off and displayed on poles or in trees. They burned people alive. They cut out their tongues. Victims who survived were enslaved and deported to cities where they were put to work on building projects. This method of operating was not short lived. It went on for more than 250 years.[8] Jonah had plenty of reason to dread these people.

It's clear to see why Jonah saw God's command as a no-win assignment. As Bruckner puts it, "Yahweh asked him to go to his cultural enemies and proclaim judgment in the capital city. . . . He was asked to risk his life preaching and had no guarantees that he would not, like other unwelcomed prophets, be killed. Yet if he succeeded in his mission and they repented, he would not be welcome in Israel."[9] Given that dilemma, Jonah runs from God.

Jonah runs, but God won't leave him alone. The Lord sends a violent storm that threatens to tear the ship apart. Is that enough of a wake-up call for Jonah? Not exactly. Even though the sailors are on deck, crying out to their own god and throwing things overboard in order to lighten the ship, Jonah is below deck, in a deep sleep. That may sound strange at first, but if you think about it a little further, it may sound uncomfortably familiar. What do people do when they're disobeying God? Admit that fact and face up to it? Or hide and pretend it's not happening? Perhaps Jonah's sleep is just another way of running from God. He is in denial, hoping the reality of his rebellion and its consequences will somehow disappear.

Jonah may be asleep, but the sailors are wide awake. Through casting lots, they figure that Jonah must be the cause of their calamity, so they confront him to find out more about who he is, where he's from, and what God he serves. He says, "I am a Hebrew and I worship the LORD, the God of heaven, who made the sea and the dry land" (Jonah 1:9). Oh, *that* God! The God who made *everything* and rules over everything and is *inescapable* because he knows exactly where Jonah is at that moment and has sent the storm that is about to kill them all. It seems absurd to flee from God, both in this story and in our own lives, yet people do it all the time. It can actually be pretty easy to live as if God doesn't see and know everything about us. Most of the time, he is so quiet, and he leaves us alone if we want him to. Occasionally, though, the circumstances of life force us to confront him, and we have to decide what we will do about him.

In that moment, Jonah tells the men to fling him into the ocean, and the sea will become calm. Is that his only option? How about crying out to the Lord, admitting he was wrong, and promising to go preach to the people of Nineveh? There is no indication that he considers that possibility. Instead, he is ready to take his punishment. He believes that he, like the Ninevites, deserves it. He believes in justice. He is willing to accept it for himself, and he believes the evil Ninevites should have to face justice too. God believes in justice, but he also believes in mercy and forgiveness, concepts that Jonah doesn't yet seem to fully accept.

Terrified as they are by their own likely destruction in the storm, the sailors don't want to follow Jonah's advice to toss him into the sea. They don't want to die, but they don't want to kill him either. They frantically try to row back to land, but the storm rages harder than ever. Finally, they realize that throwing Jonah overboard is their only hope for survival. They lift him up, and into the churning waters he goes. End of story.

Or at least it looks as if it should be the end. Usually when you throw someone into the ocean, he or she drowns. But God is not finished with any of the people in this story, not Jonah and not the sailors. How often do we find that just when it looks like the end of the story, God still has more chapters to write? Two more significant things are about to happen. As the sailors prepare to throw Jonah off the ship, you might expect that he would be the one crying out to God. Instead, he is silent, but the sailors are crying out. They beg God not to hold them responsible for taking the life of an innocent, "for you, LORD, have done as you pleased" (1:14). After Jonah is gone, and the sea grows calm, "the men greatly feared the LORD, and they offered a sacrifice to the LORD and made vows to him" (v. 16). The Lord had sent out Jonah to make converts, and unwittingly, he has done it on this ship.

As surprising as that happy outcome is, what happens next to Jonah is even more of a shock: "Now the LORD provided a huge fish to swallow Jonah, and Jonah was in the belly of the fish three days and three nights" (v. 17). I love that wording: *provided*. The fish *swallows* him. What could be more terrifying and disgusting? But that is provision. In the moment it was happening, it might not have felt overwhelmingly positive. *This is how God provides?* Yet that harrowing incident rescues Jonah from drowning. It also rescues him in the long term, since it changes his perspective—how could it not?—and allows him time to turn in obedience to God's command. In that sense, the big fish, even though we learn very little about it, offers one of the key spiritual lessons of the story: sometimes our worst ordeals are God's "great fish" sent to save us.

A Song of Gratitude from the Belly of the Fish

Now that the story has Jonah lodged safely in the belly of that fish, what I want to know is, What is it like in there? What does it smell like? Is it slimy? Do you feel as if you're going to suffocate? If I were telling the story, those are some things I would talk about. Scripture gives us none of that. Jonah is not focused on his surroundings inside that fish, as bizarre as that scenery must have been.

One thing I love about Jonah is his single-mindedness. When he picks a course of action, he is all in. When he rebels, he does it with gusto. Like many of us who have spent time in rebellion, it takes a lot to break him out of it. To break us out of our spiritual disobedience or complacency, some of us need to be shaken up in very uncomfortable ways, even if those ways are not as weird as what happens to Jonah. Otherwise, we will stay in our self-satisfied waywardness indefinitely. Jonah was about as stubbornly committed to his rebellion as you can get. The storm on the ship doesn't wake him up. The threat of being thrown overboard doesn't do it.

It takes near drowning—with the seaweed wrapped around his head, as he describes it—to make him finally call out to God for rescue.

God does rescue him, and as Jonah sits in that fish, he turns his single-mindedness toward something better than rebellion: gratitude. He chooses to concentrate on something other than the immediate troubling circumstances in which he finds himself—the gooey, dark, stifling prison of the fish's insides. He could have chosen to make that situation the subject of his song. He could freak out about this terrible joke God has played on him or the unfairness of being trapped or the likelihood that this ordeal would kill him. For any of us, when we feel trapped, oppressed, or hopeless in our current circumstances, it's easy to focus on the present and nothing else. But Jonah, for all his faults, is still able to sing a hymn of praise for how God has rescued him. He describes how the waters had engulfed him as he sank lower and lower toward the bottom of the sea. "But you, LORD my God, brought my life up from the pit" (Jonah 2:6), he says, rejoicing.

God has rescued Jonah not only physically but also spiritually. He says,
When my life was ebbing away,
    I remembered you, LORD,
and my prayer rose to you,
    to your holy temple. (V. 7)
Through his crisis, Jonah has rediscovered God's presence. He is no longer fleeing God, either physically or spiritually. He now realizes God's presence is everywhere, even in the depths of the sea or the belly of a fish. God had not found him to punish him as he deserved, but rather to save him and put him on the path to obedience. Jonah concludes his song,
Those who cling to worthless idols
    turn away from God's love for them.
But I, with shouts of grateful praise,
    will sacrifice to you.
What I have vowed I will make good.
    I will say, "Salvation comes from the LORD." (Vv. 8-9)
The ending of that song is pretty much the message God had commanded Jonah to preach to Nineveh. Does he realize it? He speaks in personal terms, of his own salvation, but the Lord wants to extend it even to the people Jonah despises. Jonah has learned about salvation, but a question remains about whether he will be willing to proclaim it once he

is back on land. Even in his gratitude for his own rescue, he doesn't say he was wrong about Nineveh. He doesn't say he now sees things the way God does. God has saved him, but the test of obedience will come once he is free from his confinement. The big fish having served its purpose now ejects Jonah onto dry land.

Jonah Finally Obeys, but . . .

The third chapter of Jonah begins, "The word of the LORD came to Jonah a second time" (v. 1). A second chance to obey! I am so grateful that God gives them. This time, Jonah does not run away. God has given him a message, and Jonah travels to Nineveh to preach it. Many of us can relate to Jonah's disobedience and fleeing from God in the first two chapters of the book, but even Jonah's obedience can sound embarrassingly familiar. He does what God says, finally, but his obedience is *grudging*. Just look at his sermon: "Forty more days and Nineveh will be overthrown" (v. 4). That's it. Or at least that's all that is recorded. This may represent only a summary of the message he brought to Nineveh, but this is not exactly the fiery prophet trying to wake up the people. He is the reluctant prophet who is ticked off with God for making him do this. He comes across like the sullen student who is forced to give a speech and therefore mumbles a perfunctory rush of words just to get the assignment over with.

Jonah's sermon cries out *not* to be listened to. It almost begs his audience not to be persuaded. He has checked off his box of obedience and can sit back and wait for the destruction.

Amazingly, and to Jonah's horror, his reluctantly delivered message of warning succeeds. The king tells everyone to call on God and stop their evil ways in the hope that God may relent. Once God sees this, he does relent. Jonah is furious. He tells God, accusingly, "Isn't this what I said, LORD, when I was still at home? That is what I tried to forestall by fleeing to Tarshish. I knew that you are a gracious and compassionate God, slow to anger and abounding in love, a God who relents from sending calamity" (4:2). Jonah's "I told you so" moment is accurate. God *is* like that! Jonah was happy about it when that love was extended to him, but he can't stand for God to show that kind of love to his enemies. He makes his own request of God: take his life. He would rather be dead.

God could have responded to this outburst in many ways. He responds with a question: "Is it right for you to be angry?" (v. 4). Jonah doesn't answer. He makes a shelter outside the city and waits to see what will happen. God had relented, but that didn't necessarily mean he would relent forever. Would the Ninevites turn back to their old sinful ways and still receive the destruction Jonah hoped for? If so, he would be there, ready to watch.

God is not finished teaching Jonah. He provides a vine to grow over Jonah's head to give shade from the blazing sun. Jonah is happy about that, just as he was happy about his rescue from the sea. But the next morning, God provides a worm that kills the vine, and Jonah finds himself once again suffering under the hot sun and a scorching wind. Never one for a mild reaction to anything, Jonah once again declares that he would rather die than live. God once again asks Jonah whether it is right for him to be angry. The chapter concludes with, "But the LORD said, 'You have been concerned about this plant, though you did not tend it or make it grow. It sprang up overnight and died overnight. And should I not have concern for the great city of Nineveh, in which there are more than a hundred and twenty thousand people who cannot tell their right hand from their left—and also many animals?'" (vv. 10-11).

Jonah cares about the vine, but only in how he benefits from it personally. God has a wider perspective. He loves all of his creation—humans, animals, plants. God is also sovereign. He can forgive. He can give second chances. He can relent when he chooses to allow for repentance and changed lives. He wants Jonah to share those compassionate values. Justice is important. God has not forgotten about it or abandoned it. God gave the Ninevites a chance to repent, which they did. However, although it is not covered in the book of Jonah, their repentance was short lived. Ultimately, as James Bruckner points out, "Nineveh was destroyed. The Ninevites' repentance did not hold very long. By the time the book made it into its final form (fifth century B.C.) and into the final biblical canon (A.D. 90), Nineveh was a distant memory (destroyed early in the seventh century B.C.)."[10]

The book of Jonah does not end with that sad news. It ends with God's question about whether Jonah thinks the Lord should have concern for the 120,000 people of Nineveh and their animals too. Jonah's response is not recorded. He is left to contemplate the question, and so are we.

It's easy to see why Jonah has been so popular over the centuries and why the story has been retold in countless ways in many genres. It's not just the big fish that makes it a remarkable story. Jonah himself turns out to be just as stubborn and contradictory and in need of God's grace as we are. Most of us can find ourselves somewhere in this story. Like Jonah, we are left wrestling not only with God's answers but also with his questions.

Notes

1. *Jonah's Big Fish Adventure*, illus. Denis Alonso, The Beginner's Bible (Grand Rapids: Zonderkidz, 2018), n.p.

2. Joyce Denham, *The Hard to Swallow Tale of Jonah and the Whale*, illus. Amanda Hall (Oxford, UK: Lion Hudson, 2015), n.p.

3. Dandi Daley Mackall, *Jonah and the Fish*, illus. Lissy Marlin, Flipside Stories (Carol Stream, IL: Tyndale House, 2016), n.p.

4. Herman Melville, *Moby-Dick; or, The Whale* (New York, 1851; Project Gutenberg, 2017), chap. 9, http://www.gutenberg.org/files/2701/2701-h/2701-h.htm.

5. Melville.

6. World History Encyclopedia, s.v. "Jonah and the Fish," illus. Sailko, last modified January 8, 2018, https://www.worldhistory.org/image/7834/jonah—the-fish/.

7. World History Encyclopedia, s.v. "Jonah and the Whale," illus. Pieter Lastman, last modified January 8, 2018, https://www.worldhistory.org/image/7835/jonah—the-whale/.

8. James Bruckner, *Jonah, Nahum, Habakkuk, Zephaniah*, The NIV Application Commentary (Grand Rapids: Zondervan, 2004), 28-29.

9. Bruckner, 30.

10. Bruckner, 126.

Digging Deeper

1. Does Jonah really believe he can successfully flee from God? He admits to the sailors on the ship that he worships "the LORD, the God of heaven, who made the sea and the dry land" (Jonah 1:9)—that is, the God who made and oversees *everything* and therefore is *inescapable*. In what ways do people flee from God today? How are they similar to the way Jonah did it? How do people convince themselves that God is not watching? What does it take to change their minds?

2. Jonah 1:17 says, "Now the LORD provided a huge fish to swallow Jonah." Note the word "provided" in that verse. Being swallowed by the fish was terrifying and disgusting, but it was also *provision*. In what ways did it serve that purpose for Jonah? This chapter says, "Sometimes our worst ordeals are God's 'great fish' sent to save us." Can you think of any examples of that from your own life? Has something bad ever turned out to also be God's provision?

3. This chapter lists versions of Jonah's story retold in books, paintings, songs, and other forms. Most of those retellings include the "whale," or big fish. However, the biblical book of Jonah includes a number of other scenes that do not include the fish. If you were asked to produce a painting that captures the essential message of Jonah but that does not include the fish, what would you paint?

Go to https://www.thefoundrypublishing.com/8OT/LeaderGuide for a free downloadable leader's guide that includes more questions for reflection as well as activities for use in a small group setting.

10

The Lord Answering Job out of the Whirlwind // William Blake // 1825

And Yet, There Is So Much More!

THE OLD TESTAMENT PASSAGES discussed throughout this book have had an incalculable impact on the world. The world's laws, stories, works of art, and individual lives have been shaped and shaken by these magnificent words. I have also been challenged and changed as I studied these passages, watched the movies that were inspired by them, read the poems that retold them, viewed the statues, toys, and other objects that imitated them, and read what biblical scholars had to say about them. I saw that almost no aspect of modern life remains untouched by these Old Testament texts.

The profound cultural impact of the Old Testament, however, does not tell the full story. These words are also deeply personal for me and for millions of other readers. What keeps me coming back to these biblical texts day after day, year after year, is not just an academic interest but also something that reaches the gut level, and a matter of spiritual survival. These words work on me in a similar way that certain songs and works of literature do, striking so deeply that they begin to seem crucial for living. These passages reveal reality and lead me to say, *yes, this is the way life really is; this is the truth.*

To think of Scripture so personally is in no way to discount crucial elements like the historical context, the text's original audience and purpose, or other scholarly concerns. The personal connection I am referring to does not *contradict* those ways of looking at the Old Testament; it is deepened by them. The point is simply that a solely scholarly approach cannot fully contain these biblical texts. The passages explode beyond that. I respect the work of biblical scholars and have leaned on them heavily as I researched and wrote this book. But what the scholars cannot do, at least by themselves, is make the passages *mine.*

The words of the Old Testament will reach the core of who I am only if I treat them as a necessary part of my identity. For me, it is analogous to how I relate to the books that I study and teach as an English professor. The great literary works that I have written about and taught for decades don't exist merely as academic subjects that I approach on a purely intellectual basis. These words ooze out of me even when I'm not intending to think about them.

When I'm going through my daily life, the literature in my mind gets triggered by all kinds of things—a remark I overhear, something I see in nature, a story I hear on the news, a post I read on social media. Any of those things can spark a line from Robert Frost, a phrase from Thomas Wolfe, a snippet of dialogue from Arthur Miller, an image from Emily Dickinson, a concept from Kierkegaard. I can't help it. That's what fills my mind because that's what I've spent my life studying. That's what I mean by the passages being mine. Wolfe and Dickinson and Frost weren't thinking about *me* when they wrote those lines. For me to connect them to my own life is, in one sense, to take them out of context. But their words live in me, a real reader, which *was* the intention of each of those authors. The words are mine in the same way that songs I love trigger memories from my own life that go far beyond the actual lyrics on the page.

In a similar way, the words of the Bible can become "mine," but there are also dangers to avoid in this way of thinking. In his book *Saving the Bible from Ourselves*, Glenn R. Paauw warns against treating Scripture as a "snacking Bible," in which we pull out our favorite little out-of-context snippets of Scripture and ignore the harder, more disturbing parts. This approach violates the meaning of Scripture and ultimately leaves us unsatisfied. He writes, "We read our little spiritual morsel and discover it doesn't nourish us all that much, and certainly not enough to carry us through the day. Actually, we kind of forget it pretty quickly."[1] Paauw urges readers to stop being satisfied with "small readings" of the Bible and instead do "big readings," which he describes as "magnified experiences that result when communities engage natural segments of texts, or whole books, taking full account of the Bible's various contexts."[2] Big readings will require lots of time, study, and commitment. Paauw writes that instead of expecting instant satisfaction, "we will give ourselves over to the Bible. With faith ultimately in the Spirit whom we believe inspired it to be the kind of book it is, we will believe that over time it will do for us all we need and more. It will feed us. It will speak to our lives now. It will be relevant. But we will come by these gifts honestly."[3]

I want the great words of the Old Testament to fill me, inspire me, and draw me closer to God, but to get there, am I willing to become a lifelong learner of it, to make it part of my everyday reading? Am I willing to read entire books of the Old Testament, even when they seem daunting and confusing? Am I ready to learn from others—fellow believers, commentators, pastors? Am I willing to read the biblical texts in community, not focusing on little portions in quick studies, but reading long sections out loud and letting the words penetrate and change me and my fellow readers? I might wish that the Old Testament offered up its meaning more easily, but it doesn't. To fully experience it, the burden is on me and my faith community to explore its meaning. The Bible will not quickly make itself "relevant" to me at a quick glance.

In my college courses, I teach difficult texts that are hundreds of years old. At first, the responses from some skeptical students to works by authors such as Boethius, Dante, or Teresa of Ávila can be frustration or confusion, even when the texts have been translated into modern English versions. Why bother with these dusty old books, with their antiquated concepts and their old-fashioned worldviews? Hasn't the world moved on? Don't we understand things better nowadays? Why not just stick with more recent authors, who understand the modern world, or, better yet, skip reading altogether and watch YouTube videos or films that communicate more efficiently and are easier to understand?

The payoff of reading the great texts is worth it, I assure my students, even though it may require a lot more work to dig it out. Students are usually grateful they have read these classic texts once they have done the work. Once the students break through the barriers of time and language, their eyes are opened to truths they could have received no other way. They see that these texts have stood the test of time for good reason. These writers, who can seem so distant at first, so alien, were people like us, struggling to make sense of reality and to write deeply and truthfully about it. They produced these works often at great personal sacrifice.

The same is true of the Bible. It's worth every minute of effort to make those words of Scripture a part of who you are. Truth is in those words. The Holy Spirit speaks through those words.

But let's face it. Long stretches of the Old Testament can seem pretty boring. I follow a regular reading plan that takes me through the Bible on a continual basis, over and over again, year after year. Sometimes I hit long sections that feel as if they are never going to end and that don't speak much to me personally in the moment that I am reading them. Maybe it's long lists of obscure laws or angry, whirling prophecies against nations that seem pretty distant from my life. What do I do about that?

I keep reading. The Old Testament isn't set up like a crime thriller or detective novel with suspenseful build-ups and plot twists to keep me constantly on the edge of my seat. It has a much wider sweep and a much greater purpose. What about those passages that seem so unduly harsh or inexplicable or incomplete? I keep reading. One thing I have learned from teaching literature for so many years is that great works do not give up their secrets all at once.

With lesser works, you can read them through once and gain pretty much all you will ever get out of them. I like to read spy novels for fun, but I rarely read them more than once. They offer most of what they have the first time through, and if I read them again, hoping for that same enjoyment, I usually feel let down. But a great work, like a Shakespeare play, for example, never stops providing a probing experience, no matter how many times I have read it or taught it. I once had a Shakespeare professor who said he had read *Hamlet* more than five hundred times, and he still wasn't finished learning from it. He said he could have memorized it by that point, but he purposely chose not to because he wanted to allow the text to speak to him fresh every time.

I love it when I reach a portion of Scripture that meant little or nothing to me in earlier readings, but now it suddenly springs to life. There have been moments when I have asked, When did they put *that* in the Bible? I don't remember ever seeing it. How could I have missed it? Why isn't everybody talking about this passage? I often switch translations when I start a new read-through of the Bible, and that alone brings the words to life in new ways. Now, when I come across sections that seem particularly obscure or frustrating, I take in what I can and move on. Some passages can be explained with help from commentators, but others I am simply not ready for. Maybe I'll understand them better a year from now or ten years from now or in eternity.

Dry, Scattered Bones Spring to Life

One passage that burst forth in a new way for me within the last few years is Ezekiel 37. That chapter had been in the Old Testament my entire life, of course. I must have read it many times over the years, but for me, it sat there lifeless, a nondescript chapter of words that left no lasting impression. But then, like the dried-up bones the chapter describes, life was suddenly breathed into it, or into my reading of it, and now for me it pulses and dances and sings with meaning. It has become one of my favorite portions of Scripture, infused with the power of the Holy Spirit.

The book of Ezekiel is in many ways a very unpleasant book, written at the time of the Babylonian exile. It's a book of prophecy, presaging judgment and destruction. It's filled with chapter after chapter of God's wrath and the reasons behind it. It envisages the destruction of Jerusalem and the destruction of the temple. It is set during one of the lowest points in Israel's history, and it includes prophecy not only against that nation but also against many others, most of which readers like me have never heard of. All in all, it's a depressing book to read. It also can get a little tedious with all those proclamations against this place and that place. Maybe that's why the book didn't leave much of an impression on me for so long. I read it politely, respectfully, but didn't fully engage.

God's ultimate plan for Israel in Ezekiel, and throughout Scripture, is restoration and salvation. That message eventually emerges in Ezekiel. By about chapter 34—it takes a long time to get there!—a more hopeful message about transformation is proclaimed. The end of that chapter says, "Then they will know that I, the LORD their God, am with them and that they, the Israelites, are my people, declares the Sovereign LORD. You are my sheep, the sheep of my pasture, and I am your God, declares the Sovereign LORD" (vv. 30-31). This more hopeful tone continues for the next few chapters, punctuated by some prophecy of the punishment of Israel's enemies. Chapter 36 contains truly beautiful passages, such as, "I will give you a new heart and put a new spirit in you; I will remove from you your heart of stone and give you a heart of flesh. And I will put my Spirit in you and move you to follow my decrees and be careful to keep my laws. Then you will live in the land I gave your ancestors; you will be my people, and I will be your God" (vv. 26-28).

Those chapters show that God has a plan of transformation and renewed relationship for Israel, and once God has delivered that message, the spirit of the Lord places Ezekiel in the middle of a valley, where he receives the stunning vision described in chapter 37. You've almost certainly heard the story, or at least the song version of it. It's about the dry bones that God puts together and brings to life. You can probably hear James Weldon Johnson's song "Dem Bones" in your head right now: "Knee bone connected to the thigh bone / Thigh bone connected to the hip bone," and so on it goes, until you get to the chorus, "Dem bones, dem bones gonna walk around. . . . Now hear the word of the Lord."[4] I had known that song since I was a child, and that was about all that stood out to me about Ezekiel. That song always sounded like a kids' song to me, lighthearted and fun, but nothing of much spiritual depth to ponder.

Then, in my Bible reading, using Eugene Peterson's *The Message* this time, I slogged through Ezekiel until I hit chapter 37. "GOD grabbed me," the chapter begins. God's Spirit sets the prophet in the middle of a desolate plain strewn with bones. "He led me around and among them—a lot of bones! There were bones all over the plain—dry bones, bleached by the sun" (vv. 1-2, MSG). As Ezekiel sits in that desolate setting, God asks a question: "Son of man, can these bones live?" (v. 3, MSG). The prophet replies, "Master GOD, only you know that" (v. 4, MSG). God tells him to prophesy over the bones and to tell the bones to listen to the message of God.

God says to them—remember, he is talking not to people, but to dry, scattered bones—"Watch this: I'm bringing the breath of life to you and you'll come to life. I'll attach sinews to you, put meat on your bones, cover you with skin, and breathe life into you. You'll come alive and you'll realize that I am GOD!" (vv. 5-6, MSG).

As strange as God's command is, requiring Ezekiel to speak to bones, the prophet obeys: "I prophesied just as I'd been commanded. As I prophesied, there was a sound and, oh, rustling! The bones moved and came together, bone to bone. I kept watching. Sinews formed, then muscles on the bones, then skin stretched over them" (vv. 7-8, MSG). Now the bodies are formed, but they still need breath, so God tells Ezekiel to prophesy, "GOD, the Master, says, Come from the four winds. Come, breath. Breathe on these slain bodies. Breathe life!" (v. 9, MSG). With those words spoken, "The breath entered them and they came alive! They stood up on their feet, a huge army" (v. 10, MSG).

It's hard to express why this story meant so much to me. There are a number of places in the Bible where dead people are brought back to life. Elijah is instrumental in raising a widow's son from the dead. Elisha also raises a boy from the dead. Jesus raises Jairus's daughter from the dead, and he raises Lazarus from the dead. Jesus himself is resurrected from the dead. The Bible tells of other examples also. But Ezekiel 37 is different from all those. Here, God places the prophet not in front of a dead *body* that needs to be resurrected. It's much more complicated. These are just bones. They are not even full, intact skeletons. They are dried, scattered bones. It's as if God is making it as difficult as possible to bring about this resurrection. Bones in the desert—impossible!

And yet, God does it. He lets Ezekiel speak the words, but it's God himself who puts the bones together, who adds the sinews, the muscles, the skin. Finally, God adds *life*—breath—as only he has the power to do. There is *nothing* God cannot revive and bring back to life. No matter how hopeless it looks, God can make it live. If he can do that with bones, then what can he do with my life? What situation is so hopeless, so dead, that he can't breathe life into it?

In the midst of that miracle, as Ezekiel looks at this huge army that has just been resurrected, God says to him, "Son of man, these bones are the whole house of Israel. Listen to what they're saying: 'Our bones are dried up, our hope is gone, there's nothing left of us'" (v. 11, MSG). But God tells Ezekiel to prophesy to them to announce their resurrection: "I'll breathe my life into you and you'll live. Then I'll lead you straight back to your land and you'll realize that I am GOD. I've said and I'll do it. GOD's Decree" (v. 14, MSG).

I got stuck on that chapter for weeks after I read it. I read it over and over. I read it to my classes. Whenever I read it out loud, I could hardly get through it—I found it so moving. This bone-resurrecting God is the one who loves us, the one we serve.

That is why I love the Old Testament. That is why I read it.

Where Were You? When a Passage Leaves You Reeling

The Old Testament is full of stories and other passages like Ezekiel 37 that rest between the covers of the book until, for whatever reason, you are ready to hear them. Maybe you just weren't paying attention before, or maybe life's circumstances have made the passage finally possible for you to understand, or maybe the Holy Spirit has been waiting for just the right time to make this passage come alive. When this happens, I often feel the need to read a passage repeatedly, over the course of weeks or months, as if my mind and soul are thirsty to absorb the truth that is there but that I haven't yet been able to fully grasp.

I have studied and even taught the book of Job for many years, including retellings of it in plays and poems. It's a book that teaches me something new every time. It also has attracted countless interpretations, and I have learned from many of those, too, even when I disagree with them or don't understand them. Job, in his suffering, wants to hear from God. He wants to know why God is treating him so horribly. Instead of answers from the Lord, Job gets chapter after chapter of explanations, accusations, speculations, and advice from his friends, not always sympathetically delivered. I had read this repeatedly over the years, but during one reading, all of that was finally overshadowed by the last several chapters of the book, when God finally responds and leaves Job—and me—reeling.

Out of a storm, God finally speaks, and when he does, the book turns from Job questioning God to God questioning Job:

Where were you when I laid the earth's foundation?

Tell me, if you understand.

Who marked off its dimensions? Surely you know!

Who stretched a measuring line across it?

On what were its footings set,

or who laid its cornerstone—

while the morning stars sang together

and all the angels shouted for joy?" (Job 38:4-7)

Where were you? Those words, which had never stood out to me in previous readings of Job, now kept coming back to mind for weeks after I read them. God, who has been silent throughout Job's long ordeal, now fires one question after another in a lengthy talk—the longest speech attributed to God in all of Scripture—and with each question, I feel more in awe of who he is and more aware of my own smallness:

Have you journeyed to the springs of the sea

or walked in the recesses of the deep?

Have the gates of death been shown to you?

Have you seen the gates of the deepest darkness?

Have you comprehended the vast expanses of the earth?

Tell me, if you know all this. (Vv. 16-18)

It is a stunning stretch of biblical poetry that goes on for four chapters, chronicling God's creative energy, his power, wisdom, and sovereignty. It's worth reading again and again. *Where were you?*

Does the hawk take flight by your wisdom
 and spread its wings toward the south?
Does the eagle soar at your command
 and build its nest on high? (39:26-27)

God is beyond my comprehension, beyond my questioning, yet I do question—I do keep seeking the answers to all the little questions and also to the big question: *Why?* Sometimes the only answer is the one found in Job. His ways are beyond me. I couldn't contain the answers even if I received them. Job had felt abandoned by God, but God was there all along, present but silent in his suffering. "Surely I spoke of things I did not understand," Job replies at the end of God's speech, "things too wonderful for me to know" (42:3).

The Old Testament remains powerfully relevant because it touches every extreme of human nature—despair, joy, hope, reverence, love, bewilderment, fear. I have been gripped by the story of Elijah under the broom tree—exhausted, emotionally spent, hungry, running from Jezebel's threat of death. Elijah has enjoyed a great triumph in the contest over the prophets of Baal, whom he destroyed as he revealed the Lord's power and ended the drought. But his victory brought about Jezebel's wrath, and he goes on the run. He asks the Lord to take his life as he lies there discouraged and afraid. But God is not finished with him. God does not take his life. Instead, he lets him sleep. Then an angel comes and gives him food. Then he sleeps some more. Then the angel wakes him up and gives him more food. God takes care of him because Elijah has a big journey ahead.

He goes to Mount Horeb, where God is going to reveal himself to Elijah. A wind so mighty that it breaks rocks in pieces comes along, but God is not in the wind. Then an earthquake comes, but God is not in the earthquake. Then a fire, but the Lord is not in the fire. Then, after the fire, comes "a gentle whisper" (1 Kings 19:12). Elijah has finally encountered the presence of God. Elijah is ready, and the Lord now sends him on his mission.

The number of passages that have shaken me are almost endless. I remember a time when Ecclesiastes suddenly glowed bright in my mind, and I read it repeatedly and even memorized portions. Certain psalms have emerged that way, and so did portions of Jeremiah. I know people for whom passages from Genesis, Esther, Proverbs, Isaiah, Lamentations, Daniel, and Habakkuk have been life changing. You may be able to add others to this list. As we keep reading, what new passages might emerge that had never stood out before? I don't want to miss them.

Whenever I reach the end of a literature course I am teaching, I tell the students that I will consider the course a success and will believe it has fulfilled its mission if they do one thing: keep reading more of the literature on their own. Sometimes they really do. Sometimes, years later, they tell me about it. I have the same hope for readers of this book. No matter what details from these chapters you may remember or forget, if this book pushes you back to those incomparable texts of the Bible, then that is enough for me.

Notes

1. Glenn R. Paauw, *Saving the Bible from Ourselves: Learning to Read and Live the Bible Well* (Downers Grove, IL: IVP Books, 2016), 15.

2. Paauw, 11.

3. Paauw, 69.

4. Wikipedia, s.v. "Dem Bones," last modified March 16, 2021, 01:33, https://en.wikipedia.org/wiki/Dem_Bones; Wikipedia, s.v. "James Weldon Johnson," last modified May 18, 2021, 20:19, https://en.wikipedia.org/wiki/James_Weldon_Johnson.

Digging Deeper

1. The author discusses how *personal* the Old Testament texts are for him. They have had a huge impact on the wider culture, but he also thinks of them as necessary for spiritual survival. They have become a part of who he is. What is your own *personal* connection to the Old Testament? What would you like it to be?

2. Do you agree with this chapter's point that there are some passages of the Bible that we are not personally ready for yet? Can you think of biblical passages that once seemed incomprehensible, dull, or irrelevant to you but that later burst forth with greater meaning and significance?

3. If you were to add another chapter to this book examining the influence of an Old Testament passage, what passage would you add and why?

Go to https://www.thefoundrypublishing.com/8OT/LeaderGuide for a free downloadable leader's guide that includes more questions for reflection as well as activities for use in a small group setting.

Acknowledgments

Writing a book is not easy. Whenever I am working on one, I always reach a point, usually around 2:00 a.m. on some random night in the middle of the process, when I wake up in a panic and think, *I can't do this! What was I thinking?* In that moment, I feel ready to quit, crawl in a hole, and never be seen or heard from again. Then the morning comes, the light reappears, the ideas start to flow, and the words somehow follow. This is my eleventh book, and the longer I write, the more I realize how much I depend on the love and support of family, friends, colleagues, and readers to keep me on track. There isn't room to thank everyone I should thank, but I still need to mention a few by name.

I want to thank my wife, Peggy, for her love and support and for putting up with all my writerly quirks. Thanks to our children, Jacob and Katie, who motivate me and make me proud. I thank my dad and my sister, Debbie, for their love and encouragement over the years.

I am grateful to my Christian prayer group of artists and writers, called the Ninos, who have prayed me through every book for the past twenty-two years. I thank my friends in the Sunday school class I teach at Glendora Community Church for their prayers and encouragement. I thank our pastor, Mike Platter, for his encouragement and insightful messages.

I am grateful for my students and colleagues at Azusa Pacific University, where I have taught for almost thirty years. I was given a semester-long sabbatical and a Center for Research on Ethics and Values (CREV) grant to give me time to write this book. Thanks to my department chair, Dr. Windy Petrie, and my dean, Dr. Denise Edwards-Neff, for their support of my writing. Associate Dean Dr. Joshua Canada has also been especially helpful in getting the word out about my previous book, *12 New Testament Passages That Changed the World*, which is a companion to this book.

I thank my outstanding agent, Steve Laube, for his support and wise counsel throughout my writing life. I thank the great people at The Foundry Publishing for all their good work and support, especially Bonnie Perry, Rene McFarland, Rachel McPherson, Richard E. Buckner, and others.

About the Author

Joseph Bentz, PhD, MA, is the author of *12 New Testament Passages That Changed the World* (2019, available at thefoundrypublishing.com) and six other books on Christian living. He is also the author of four novels. Bentz is professor of American literature at Azusa Pacific University in Azusa, California, where he also serves as a faculty fellow in the Honors College. He speaks and teaches nationwide. Bentz lives with his wife in Southern California. They have two children. More information about his books and speaking is available at his website, josephbentz.com.